A New Approach to Accuracy & Organization for Quilters

# easy Precision PIECING

Shelley Scott-Tobisch

C&T PUBLISHING

**PUBLISHER:** Amy Marson

**CREATIVE DIRECTOR:** Gailen Runge

**ACQUISITIONS EDITOR:** Roxane Cerda

**MANAGING EDITOR:** Liz Aneloski

**EDITOR:** Lynn Koolish

**TECHNICAL EDITOR:** Debbie Rodgers

**COVER/BOOK DESIGNER:** April Mostek

**PRODUCTION COORDINATOR:** Zinnia Heinzmann

**PRODUCTION EDITOR:** Alice Mace Nakanishi

**ILLUSTRATOR:** Linda Johnson

**PHOTO ASSISTANT:** Mai Yong Vang

**STYLE PHOTOGRAPHY** by Lucy Glover and **INSTRUCTIONAL PHOTOGRAPHY** by Mai Yong Vang of C&T Publishing, Inc., unless otherwise noted

Published by C&T Publishing, Inc., P.O. Box 1456, Lafayette, CA 94549



Library of Congress Cataloging-in-Publication Data

Names: Scott-Tobisch, Shelley, 1963- author.

Title: Easy precision piecing : a new approach to accuracy & organization for quilters / Shelley Scott-Tobisch.

Description: Lafayette, CA : C&T Publishing, Inc., 2018.

Identifiers: LCCN 2017046832 | ISBN 9781617455834 (soft cover)

Subjects: LCSH: Patchwork. | Machine sewing. | Patchwork--Patterns. | Quilting--Patterns.

Classification: LCC TT835 .S35927 2018 | DDC 746.46/041--dc23

LC record available at https://lccn.loc.gov/2017046832

Printed in China

10 9 8 7 6 5 4

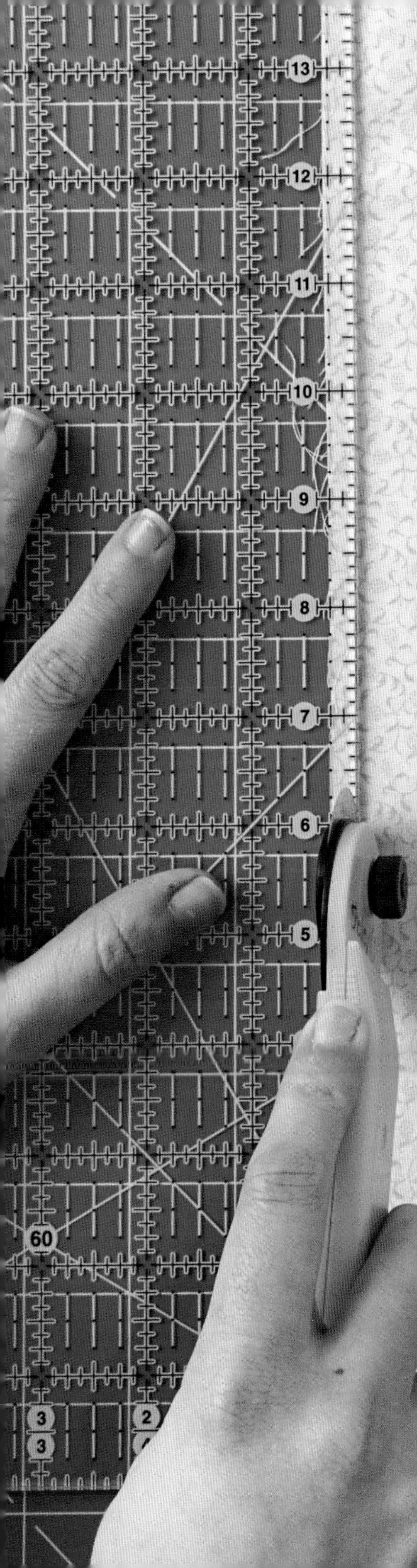

## DEDICATION

*Dedicated to my husband, Bernie. A fella can get married and become a husband. It takes heart, caring, and compassion to be a true friend.*


## ACKNOWLEDGMENTS

I would like to thank the wonderful staff at C&T Publishing for the opportunity to write *Easy Precision Piecing*. Thank you for your tireless support and patience while writing this book.

To Kimberly Jolly at Fat Quarter Shop, thank you for generously donating the beautiful Baltimore Blues bundles and precuts and to FreeSpirit Fabrics for the contribution of fabric and notions. Thank you also to Suzanne Wenzlick of Suzanne's Art House for the lovely rotary cutter charms.

Thank you to my students, past and present, for all your encouragement, questions, and suggestions—you have made me a better teacher.

I am indebted to my treasured friends who set aside time from their busy schedules to make quilts for me. To my dear friend and FBFF Carrie Lakatos who made *Song of Friendship* (page 82) and *Plum Pudding* (page 78) while running a household with two young children. To Ione MacLennan who made *Muskrat Hollow* (page 86) for her grandson and put off giving it to him so I could include her quilt in this book. To Pat Haslop who in spite of a last-minute call was able to find time to make *Sawmill Bay* (page 75). To Lauren Tolhurst and Faith McLeod for their talents and skillful quilting of the quilts. Without the efforts of all of you, the beautiful quilts in this book would not exist.

To my dear friend Sue Rogers (a.k.a. "Sandbox Sue"), thank you for teaching me about color, color families, and how to gain further understanding by putting theory into practice while dyeing fabric. I treasure our magical Sandbox Days.

To my chef, sewing machine technician, husband, and best friend, Bernie Tobisch. Thank you for the delicious meals, for keeping Gracie in tip-top condition, and for all your support.

It takes a village to write a book and I am so grateful that each and every one of you is a part of my village. Thank you.

Love, *Shelley*

# CONTENTS



## the PROJECTS

# *the* PROJECTS

# INTRODUCTION *to the* EASY PRECISION PIECING SYSTEM

- ☑ Does your ruler slip when cutting?
- ☑ Do your strips have the dreaded V at the fold?
- ☑ Do your seams not line up no matter how hard you try?
- ☑ Do your pieces mysteriously get sewn in the wrong order?
- ☑ Do you ever wonder which direction to press seams in your blocks?
- ☑ Does your fabric pop up at the seam after pressing?

If you answered yes to any of these questions, the Easy Precision Piecing System is for you. Learn about new tools and techniques for cutting, piecing, and pressing that effortlessly lead to precision. With a few simple steps, master the fine art of rotary cutting strips, squares, and triangles with ease. Find new information about thread, needles, stitch length, and the patchwork seam that naturally improve accuracy. Discover Quilt Block Builders—block blueprints with pressing arrows—and learn how to use them while piecing to keep your units organized and seams pressed for optimal results.

The Easy Precision Piecing System has a few guidelines, involves organization, planning, and new techniques for improved accuracy. These new, simple-to-adapt, skill-building techniques will appeal to all quilters from modern to traditional and beginner to expert. It is presented in a step-by-step, simple-to-understand format. Also included is valuable information on adding borders that hang straight and a new technique for easy mitered binding.

## HOW TO USE THIS BOOK

Read about the system (Quilt Block Builders and Quilt Block Bases, page 7), and then read on for all the techniques you need to be successful. Even if you are an experienced quiltmaker, I encourage you to look through the entire book before you begin a project. At the end of the book are six projects for you to try out your newfound precision piecing skills.

**NOTE: Precision Piecing Keys**

*Throughout you'll see special sections called Precision Piecing Keys. These are tips and techniques that are keys to successful precision piecing. I encourage you to pay particular attention to these sections.*

*I am so pleased to be able to share this innovative technique with you in this book. I hope it brings you as much joy and success in your quiltmaking as it has brought to me.*

# QUILT BLOCK BUILDERS *and* QUILT BLOCK BASES

*Before you get into all the details of how you can sew more precisely than ever, this chapter presents an overview of the Easy Precision Piecing System. For more details on making blocks using the Quilt Block Builders, see Making Precision-Pieced Blocks (page 53).*

The Easy Precision Piecing System is a piecing blueprint for auditioning, sewing, and storing patchwork blocks. The two major components are Quilt Block Builders (below) and Quilt Block Bases (page 8).

## QUILT BLOCK BUILDERS

Quilt Block Builders are grayscale copies of pieced blocks showing the placement of the dark and light/main and background fabrics. The Quilt Block Builder is printed larger than the finished block. You can place all your cut pieces directly on the Quilt Block Builder to audition your fabric selections. It is *not* a tool for measurement of cut pieces, only a fabric placement and pressing guide. Your finished blocks will be smaller than the printed Quilt Block Builder. The arrows on each Quilt Block Builder indicate the direction to press the seams. There are also blank circles that you color in to match with color-coded clips (see Positioning Circles, page 10, and Color-Coded Clips, page 16) to help keep patchwork in the correct position. Each different type and size of block in a quilt has its own Quilt Block Builder.

Quilt Block Builders that are larger than standard size paper can be printed in pieces and taped together or taken to a copy shop to be printed on bigger paper.

In other words, a Quilt Block Builder is both a piecing blueprint and a system of organization.

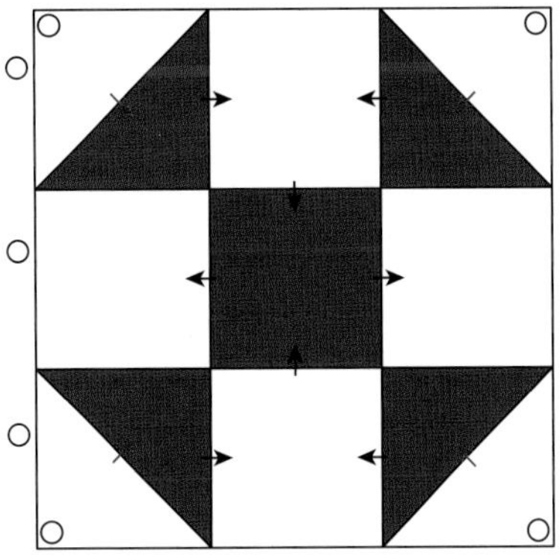

Quilt Block Builder

**Block Builders Included!**

*Quilt Block Builders are included in the book for you to copy and use for practice and projects.*

## QUILT BLOCK BASES

Quilt Block Bases consist of hard, lightweight surfaces with a sheet of see-through stabilizer of the same size fastened at the top. A Quilt Block Base is larger than the Quilt Block Builders, so the Quilt Block Builders can be inserted under the stabilizer. In essence, it is a mini design wall and a way to store blocks.

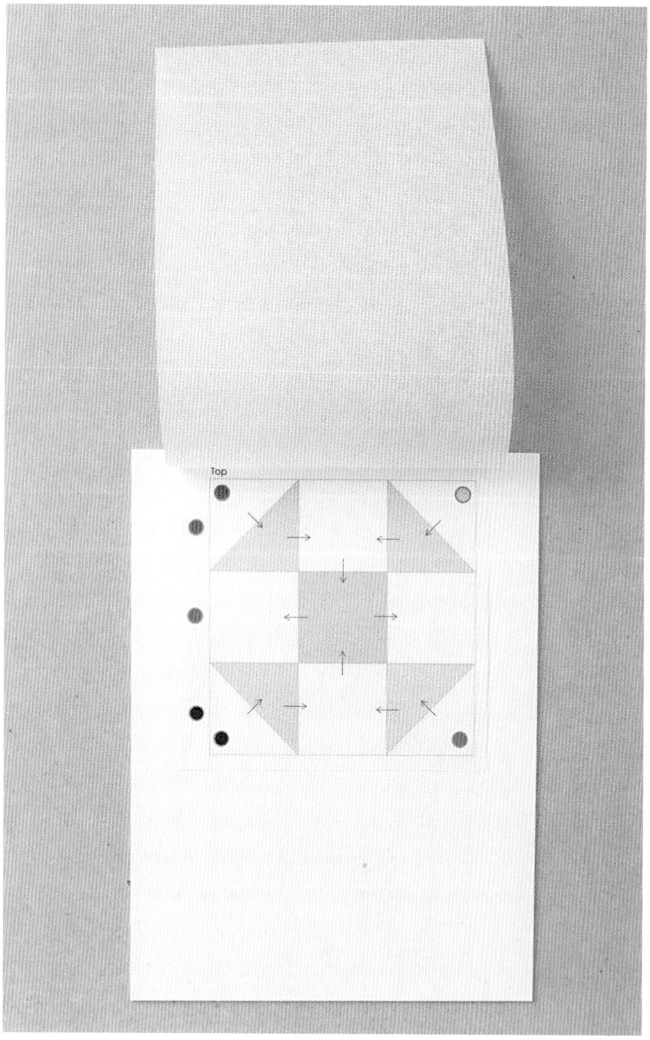


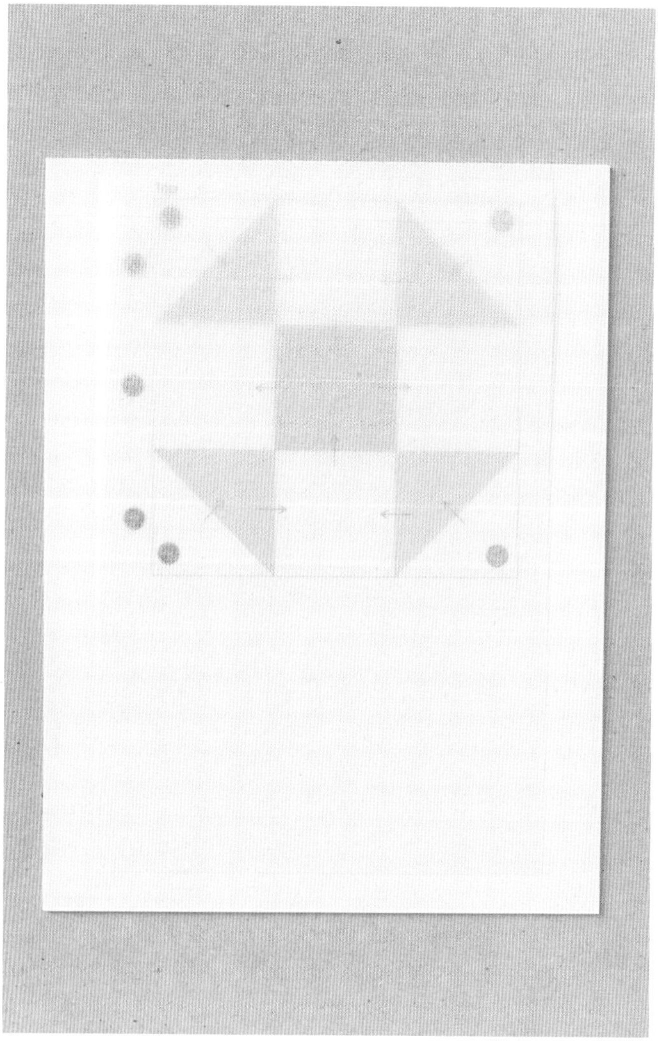

Quilt Block Builder on Quilt Block Base. The see-through stabilizer (page 17) on top of the Quilt Block Builder gently holds the patchwork pieces so they will not slide around when moving the block from cutting area to sewing machine to pressing station, like a portable mini design wall.

---

**NOTE:** *Quilt Block Bases may be purchased at my website (page 103).*

---

### How to Make Quilt Block Bases

Make your own Quilt Block Bases by cutting cardboard, foam core board, or similar material, 2″ larger than the finished block size. Cut a piece of see-through stabilizer (page 17) the same size and tape it to the top of the Quilt Block Base. Photocopy the Quilt Block Builder and slip it under the stabilizer.

## ADVANTAGES OF THE EASY PRECISION PIECING SYSTEM

- Sometimes life gets in the way and you must put your project aside for a while. It can be daunting to pull a jumble of patchwork pieces out of a drawer, a bin, or a bag and try to figure out where you left off. When you open your bin of Quilt Block Builders everything is organized and you will know right away where to begin (see Storage Bins, page 29).
- Have you ever chain pieced and opened up the blocks only to find that you have sewn the wrong edges together? Quilt Block Builders with their positioning circles and color-coded clips make this common mistake a thing of the past.
- When making scrappy blocks, use the Quilt Block Builder design board to audition fabrics. Place each fabric in position on the Quilt Block Builder and step back to view. You can add and remove pieces effortlessly and see how well they are working together before ever sewing them into a block.
- The top of the block is marked on each Quilt Block Builder. Make sure to keep "Top" up for the orientation of directional prints and the direction to press seams.
- Control the orientation of directional prints. When you use directional prints in your blocks, place them facing in the desired direction on the Quilt Block Builder and they will stay that way through the entire piecing process.
- Treat each block as if it were a quilt. Audition each individual piece using the Quilt Block Builder as a mini design wall.

## QUILT BLOCK BUILDER AS A BLUEPRINT

### Fabric Placement

Using the Shoo Fly block as an example, on a Quilt Block Builder, the main print is shown in gray and the background is white.

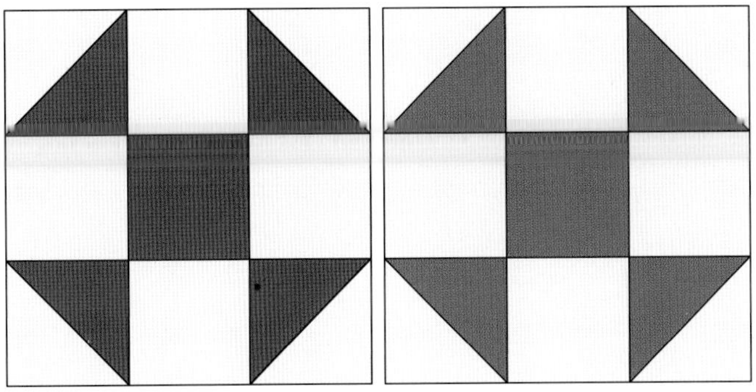

Shoo Fly block

When illustrated in gray scale, the main design stands out due to the contrast in value. This makes it easy to imagine and interpret the block in any color. When auditioning fabrics, place the main prints over the gray and background prints over the white.

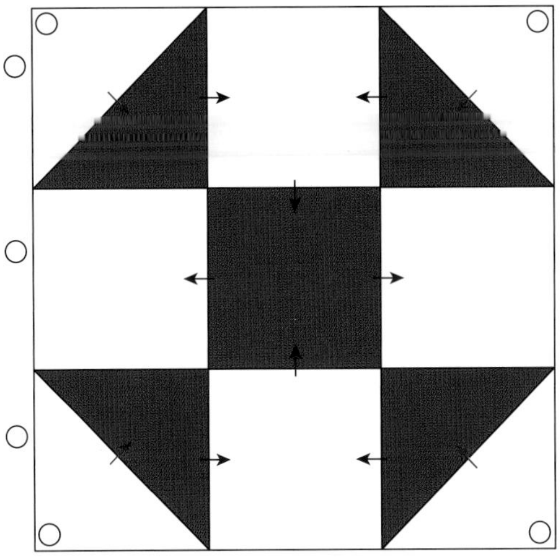


Shoo Fly Quilt Block Builder

## Positioning Circles

When you look at the Quilt Block Builder you will notice blank circles along the edges of the block. These circles are called *positioning circles*. You color them in to match color-coded clips (page 16), and together they help you put the block together properly.

## Pressing Direction

To get flat, precise blocks, it's best to nest seams whenever you can. Quilt Block Builders have arrows indicating the best direction to press the seams. This greatly improves overall appearance, accuracy, ease of piecing, and subsequent quilting (because the quilt top is flatter).

In addition to the pressing arrows, in some blocks where a number of seams come together, you'll see a bold X that indicates seams should be fanned or swirled (see Fanning Seams, page 56).

**X** A bold X in the center of four intersecting seams symbolizes fanning seams.

# MAKING MULTIPLE BLOCKS USING QUILT BLOCK BUILDERS

As a quilter, you probably make more than one block at a time. I suggest making up to ten blocks at a time using ten copies of the Quilt Block Builder and ten Quilt Block Bases. To keep track of each block, put a unique identifying sticker on the bottom center of each Quilt Block Base. Use the same sticker, on the wrong side of the fabric, to identify individual patchwork pieces that belong to that Quilt Block Builder. This way, you'll never mix up the pieces.

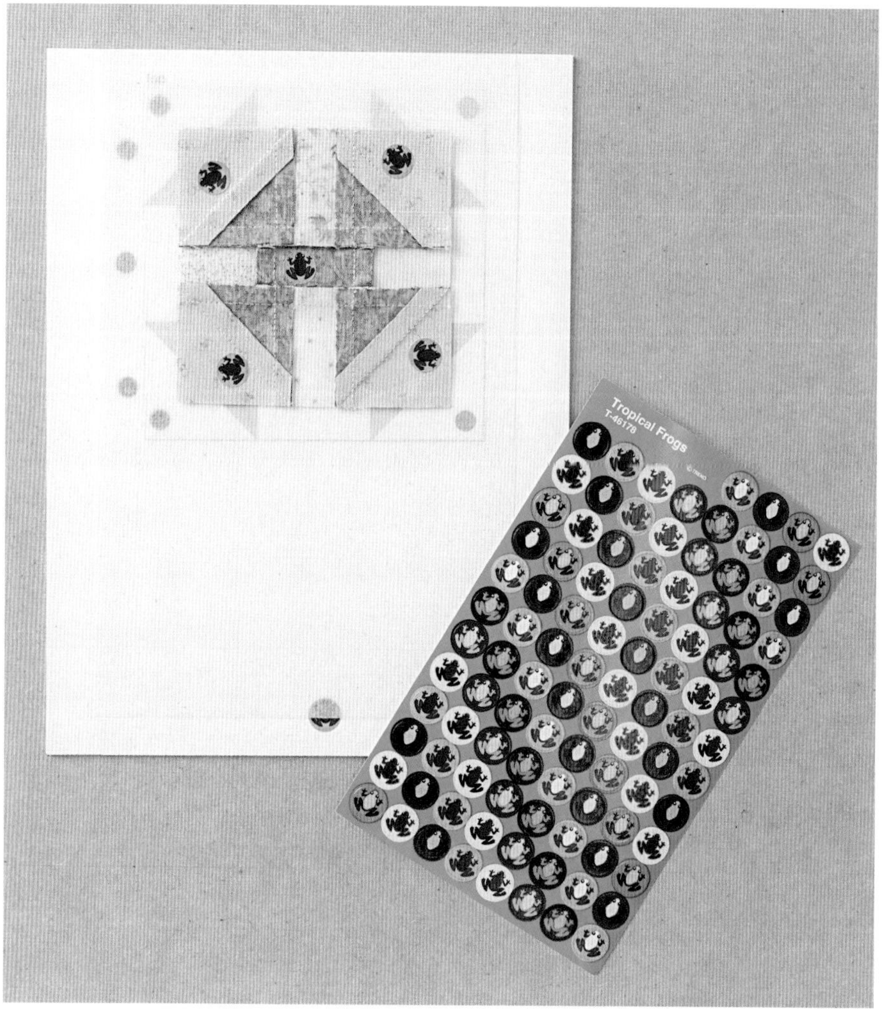


Use stickers to keep track of block pieces.

My husband claims that Quilt Block Builders saved his life. I was working on several Muskrat Paw blocks, which have 32 pieces each. He accidentally knocked three Muskrat Paw Quilt Block Builders and all their pieces onto the floor. Because of the color-coded positioning circles, color-coded clips, and stickers he was able to place all the pieces back into position, on the correct Quilt Block Builders and walk away with dignity intact.

# PRECISION PIECING TOOLS, NOTIONS, *and* SUPPLIES

## SEWING MACHINE

I used to sell sewing machines for a living. I loved helping quilters find a machine that best fit their requirements. Some with an endless budget were searching for a top-of-the-line, computerized embroidery machine. Others on a specific budget searched for a previously loved mechanical machine with a strong motor and good-quality stitch. If you are currently searching for a new or new-to-you sewing machine, I strongly recommend purchasing a machine from a dealer in your area. You might find a machine at a better price online or in a discount warehouse store, but remember that you might need help learning how to use your new machine or run into a problem that requires a sewing machine technician. Build a good relationship with a local dealer who will help you find the best machine for your needs. Make sure to test-drive the machine before making that important purchase.

Your sewing machine creates the stitches that become the backbone of your piecing. You do not need a top-of-the-line machine for precision piecing. A machine that provides balanced thread tension, even feeding, and can easily climb seams is what's essential.

Being able to control the speed is also important. Sometimes when climbing seams or matching points, you will want to slow down and do one stitch at a time; or if you are strip piecing you may want to stitch faster. A strong motor to drive the needle through layers when piecing and quilting is necessary. Availability of attachments such as a ¼″ patchwork foot and a straight-stitch plate are also things to consider. Extras such as a free-hand system (a knee-operated lever that allows you to raise and lower the presser foot without using your hands) and a needle-up/down function are added bonuses.

Take care of your machine by cleaning and oiling it regularly. This not only prolongs the life of your machine it also improves performance. Get out your manual. Learn where to oil and which parts you can remove for cleaning.

Get your machine serviced regularly by a sewing machine technician. Depending on how often you use your machine every year or two is good.

---

**NOTE:** *I sew on a BERNINA 770. Her name is Gracie. Yes, I name my machines. We spend a lot of time together and have built up a good relationship. I clean and oil my machine each time I change the needle, which is about every 6–8 hours of regular sewing. As long as I change the needle and clean and oil her regularly, Gracie gracefully handles all my precision piecing needs.*

---

# Precision Patchwork Accessories

## ¼″ Patchwork Foot

The ¼″ patchwork foot is specifically created for straight stitching. It has a flat underside and will feed your fabric evenly. Using the edge of the foot as a guide provides an accurate ¼″ seam allowance with the needle in the center position.

It is essential for the patchwork foot to cover the feed dogs for proper feeding of the fabric. It should only pivot from front to back for climbing seams, not wobble from side to side. The opening between the toes of the foot needs to be narrow enough to accommodate the needle yet wide enough to provide a view to the needle.

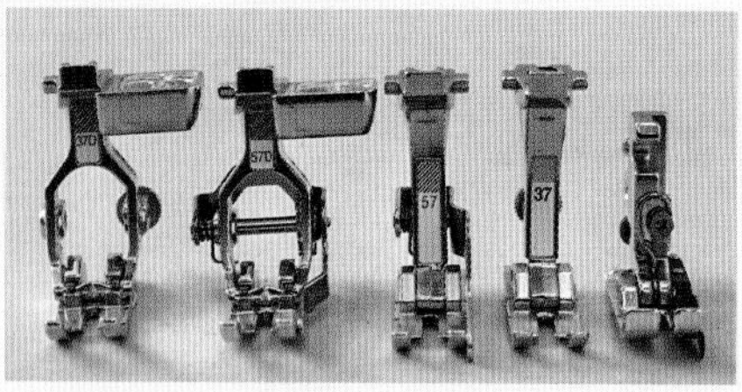
¼″ patchwork feet

### *¼″ Patchwork Foot and Feed Dogs*

Some sewing machines have feed dogs that are close together while others are farther apart. For this reason, several different styles of patchwork feet are available. Some patchwork feet are narrow both on the right and left for feed dogs that are closer together. Others are narrow only on the right and wider on the left for feed dogs that are farther apart. For precision piecing, proper feeding of the fabric is essential. If your patchwork foot is too narrow and does not at minimum cover the left feed dogs, your fabric will pucker, you will not achieve an even stitch length, and your seam allowance will vary, particularly at the beginning and end of the seam.

Many new machines come with a patchwork foot made specifically for that machine. If you do not have a patchwork foot, purchase one online or from your local dealer. You will need to know the make and model to get the correct foot for your machine.

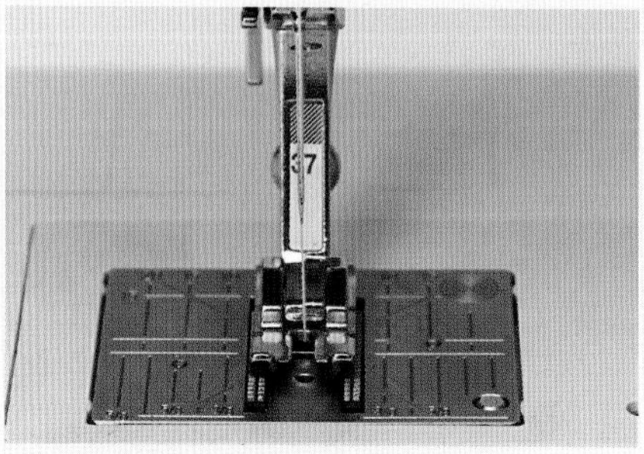
Feed dogs line up perfectly under the presser foot.

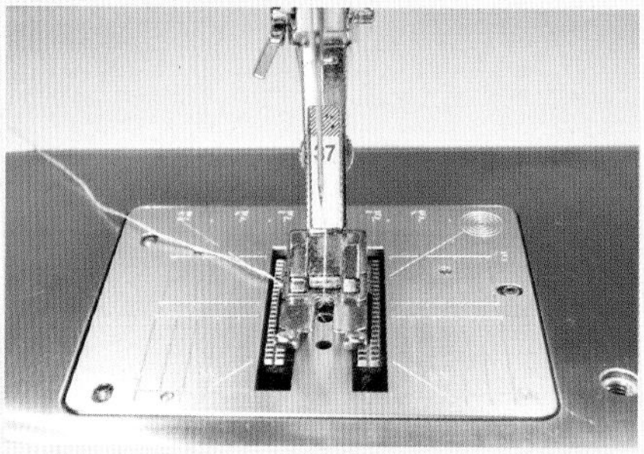
Feed dogs do not come into contact with the presser foot.

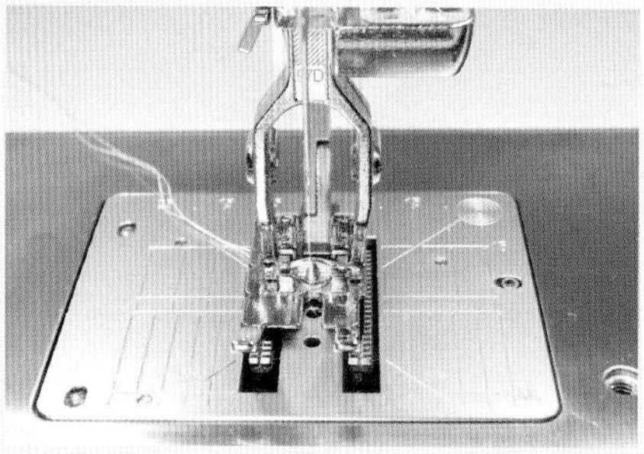
Presser foot is wider on the left side of the foot and rests on top of the feed dogs.

## Straight-Stitch Plate

The stitch plate that comes with your machine is made specifically for that particular model. It covers the bobbin area, has slots that expose the feed dogs along with an oval opening large enough to accommodate the widest stitch possible, up to 9 mm on some machines. This oval opening is necessary for decorative stitching, but when straight stitching with the needle in the center position, small pieces of fabric can get pushed down into it.

A straight-stitch plate has a small circular opening just large enough to accommodate the needle in the center position so fabric is supported all around the needle and cannot be pushed down into the small opening. When combined with the patchwork foot, this dynamic duo provide more control, better stitch quality, and easier precision piecing.

Straight-stitch plates

## PRESSING TOOLS

### PRECISION PIECING KEY: Use a Dry Iron

I do not recommend using a steam iron for patchwork. Steam can stretch and distort fabric. Patchwork corners can get stuck in steam holes and become scrunched and crinkled up.

Use a dry iron for precision pressing. My favorite iron is Continental Electric's Dry Iron. This iron heats up fast, has no auto shutoff, and is a good weight. The edge is well defined and it has a smooth flat surface so no marks are left behind when pressing fabrics and blocks. Starch does not stick to it and it is easy to clean.

Dry iron for pressing

### Pressing Surfaces

A hard, smooth, solid, and stable pressing surface is a must for a good, flat press. My large ironing board is 60″ × 20″. It is made from a sheet of ½″-thick board, is covered with a thin batting and light-colored fabric, and is attached to four legs that can be adjusted to any height. This pressing surface is ideal for pressing yardage and other large pieces of fabric. My small pressing surface is 18″ × 35″. It has a clamp on one end and an adjustable leg on the other. I attach it to my sewing machine table to the left of my machine. This ironing board accommodates my 12″ rotary mat and is used when working on small patchwork pieces.

**TIP** My ironing boards were custom made to fit my requirements by Bob Marr at Wineberry Fabrics (wineberryfabrics.com), but they also have standard models available for sale.

Sewing and pressing stations

Photo by Linda Marr

### Appliqué Pressing Sheet

Use an appliqué or nonstick pressing sheet (see Block Assembly Pressing Station, page 51) to protect the ironing board cover from repeated pressing, starching, and gluing. I prefer the ones made by Bear Thread Designs (bearthreaddesigns.com).

## ROTARY CUTTING TOOLS

Today's rotary cutting tools make it easy to accurately cut through several layers of fabric.

### Rotary Cutter

When I first started quilting 27 years ago, I was aware of only the OLFA 45 mm cutter, so this is the cutter I grew up with. Over the years I have tried many other brands, styles, and sizes, yet for comfort and precision I still prefer the standard OLFA 45 mm to all the others. I recommend trying out a few different rotary cutters to find the one that works best for you.

### Rulers

Many different styles and brands of acrylic rulers are made specifically for rotary cutting. Omnigrid, OLFA, and Creative Grids are my go-to rulers. These rulers are printed on the bottom with extreme accuracy and give trusted measurements. OLFA Frosted Advantage rulers are printed with narrow black lines and are very easy to read. Creative Grids Itty-Bitty Eights rulers (designed by Lisa Bongean of Primitive Gatherings) have a nonslip grid on the back and are clearly marked with black lines, making these rulers wonderful for small, accurate cuts. Both brands of rulers are marked in 1″ and ⅛″ increments. For OLFA, the sizes I use the most are the 6″ × 24″, 6″ × 12″, and 6″ or 6½″ squares. Many more sizes are available on the market, but these are good to start with. The Itty-Bitty Eights rulers are available in three sizes: 5″ × 15″, 3″ × 7″, and 6½″ × 6½″. I highly recommend all three sizes for precision cutting small pieces; I use all three of them equally.

**TIP** Omnigrid makes a 4″ × 14″ ruler that is ideal for folding and storing fabrics (see Cutting and Folding for Starching and Storage, page 28).

### Mats

Rotary cutting mats are self-healing mats that are usually marked on one side and solid on the other. These mats have a smooth cutting surface that will not dull the blade. For working at home and for large cuts, I prefer an OLFA or Omnigrid 24″ × 36″ mat. When making smaller cuts and traveling, I prefer a 12″ × 18″ mat. The OLFA 17″ × 17″ and 12″ × 12″ rotary mats are my favorite mats for smaller cuts and traveling.

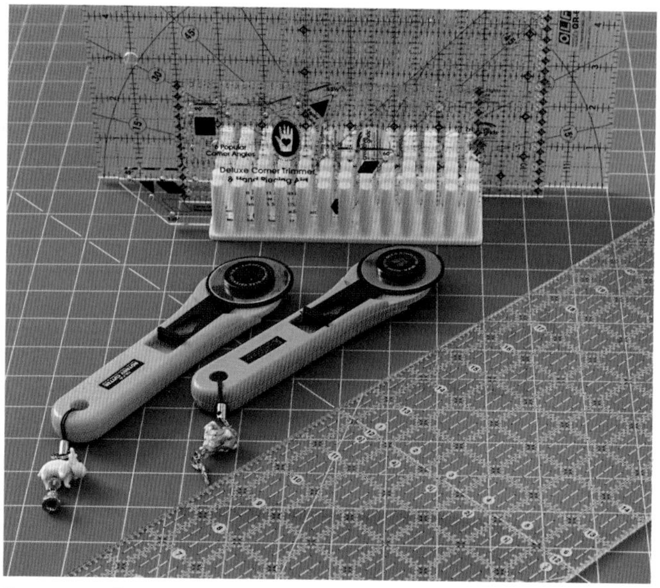

Rotary cutting equipment with Poppin's Softie Grip Grass to hold rulers—this product is designed to hold office supplies but works great for cutting tools.

**TIP** **Mat Maintenance**

To prolong the life of your mats, keep them out of direct sunlight and extreme hot and cold. When cutting, use a sharp blade as dull blade can cut deep, wide grooves in the mat that cannot heal. Store flat and on occasion give mats a good wash with tepid water and mild detergent.

**PRECISION PIECING KEY:**

## Use the Same Ruler for Consistent Cutting

For consistency in precision cutting, I usually recommend using only the same brand ruler, but I have found that I can use the OLFA 6″ × 24″ and 6″ × 12″ rulers for long and short cuts and the trio of Itty-Bitty Eights rulers for small cuts and subcuts. These rulers work well together and provide supreme accuracy.

## SMALL TOOLS

### Scissors

Scissors come in a variety of sizes and styles depending on your cutting, snipping and trimming needs. Good quality, sharp scissors make your job easier. I prefer Dovo, Kai, and Gingher.

### Tweezers

Tweezers are great tools to have on hand for pulling out tiny bits of thread left over from removing a seam and for holding onto little patchwork units. My favorite tweezers are Apliquick Ergonomic Sewing Tweezers. They have a wide base and beveled points for a firm grip. These tweezers are as attractive as they are functional.

### Seam Ripper

Removing seams can be unnerving enough without having to fight to get your seam ripper under the stitches. Do yourself a favor and purchase a good quality seam ripper with a small pointed tip and sharp blade. Maybe even a fancy one to make seam ripping almost enjoyable. When removing stitches from long seams such as borders, I prefer to use an OLFA Technic Knife.

#### *¼″ Marking Tool*

Marking a ¼″ from the edge of the binding is important for making tidy miters in the corners of binding. For easy ¼″ marking, I prefer to use a Deluxe Corner Trimmer (by From Marti Michell, frommarti.com). (For more on binding, see Binding, page 98.)

---

## NOTIONS AND SUPPLIES

### Cotton Thread

For precision piecing, I recommend 100% cotton long staple DMC 50/2 or Aurifil thread. These threads are fine, strong, and create very little lint.

Select a thread color that matches or blends with the lightest-color fabric in your quilt. If you are making a quilt with high contrast, such as black and white, choose a white thread. The stitches will look nicer and will not shadow through the white fabric. For traditional-style quilts with a light background, I work with DMC color 712 Cream or Aurifil color 2309 Silver White.

The numbering system for thread has two parts: weight and ply. *Weight*, the first number, refers to the thickness of the thread. The *higher* the number, the *thinner* the thread. For example, 100-weight thread is thin, while 12-weight is thick. *Ply*, the second number, refers to the number of strands twisted together to form that thread. On a spool labeled 50/2, 50 is the weight and 2 is the number of strands twisted together to form that thread.

Light-colored DMC and Aurifil threads for piecing

If a spool of thread is labeled only with the weight, such as Cotton 50 or Ne 50, it will most often be a 2-ply thread. If you are uncertain how many plies are in a thread, untwist the thread until you can see the individual strands.

## Needles

For best results use a needle with a sharp point for precision piecing.

For piecing, I prefer HLx5 DP (durable point) hard chrome needles (by Organ Needle Company), size 70/10 or 80/12. (I prefer Organ brand, but other brands make this type of needle too.) These are industrial needles cut with a flat shank for use in domestic machines. They have a very sharp point for good stitch quality. They are stronger and more rigid than regular needles—there is less chance of needle deflection and they last nearly twice as long. Microtex (sharps) needles are also a good choice for precision piecing—these needles have a long tapered sharp point and produce great stitch quality. They may need to be replaced more often as the tapered point can be more easily damaged.

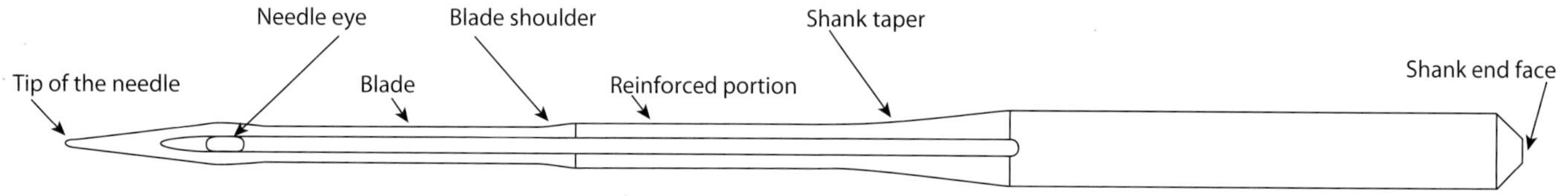


The anatomy of a sewing machine needle

Most needle companies print both European and Imperial sizes on a package of needles. To help remember what the numbers represent it is easiest to memorize that a 100/16 = 1 mm in diameter, 90/14 = 0.9 mm, and so on. The larger the number, the bigger the needle.

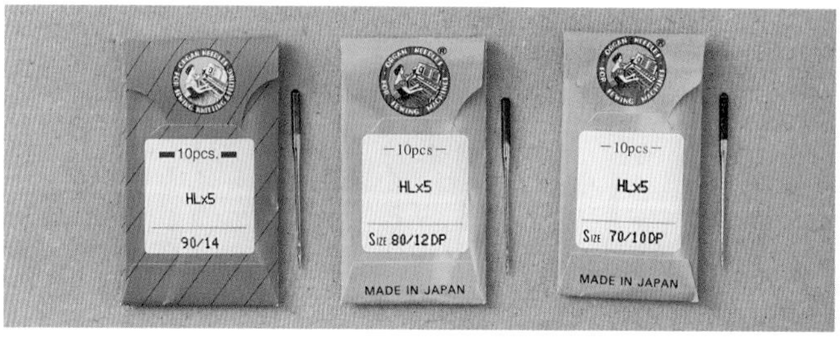


Sewing machine needles for piecing

**PRECISION PIECING KEY:**

## Selecting the Correct Needle Size

When choosing which size needle to use for your project, keep in mind the weight of thread and quality of stitches. Test different sizes of needles. Use a needle that does not skip stitches when going over multiple seams and produces a good quality stitch. Use a bigger needle if the stitches are wavy, crooked, or skipping. Use a smaller needle if the resulting needle hole is too large for the thread to fill.

**TIP** **When to Put in a New Sewing Machine Needle**

A needle will last about 6–8 hours of sewing and the tip will become blunt or bent over time. If you hear a popping sound, change your needle. The blunt, bent end of a needle can damage both your fabric and machine.

## Color-Coded Clips

Color-coded clips are used along with basting glue (page 43) for matching seams and points. They are also used with Quilt Block Builders (page 59, bottom left photo) to help keep your pieces organized.

## Basting Glue

Basting glue is a great way to hold fabric in position for sewing and effortlessly releases when needed to remove seams or press seams open. I prefer SeamAlign Gentle Hold Fabric Glue. It is safe, nontoxic, and washable. It goes on clear and dries clear.

**NOTE:** *To order Quilt Block Builders, Quilt Block Bases, SeamAlign Gentle Hold Fabric Glue, Easy Press Solution, and Easy Press Pen, see my website (page 103).*

## Starch Alternative

A lightweight starch alternative applied to seams before pressing makes the seams lie flat like magic, making it easy to sew and rotary cut large and small units alike. I prefer Easy Press Fabric Treatment by Acorn Precision Piecing Products (page 46) for pressing yardage and applying directly to seams.

Starter Kit with Easy Press Fabric Treatment, Seam Align Glue and an Easy Press Pen.

### *Starch Alternative Applicator*

Use a starch alternative applicator pen or paintbrush to apply starch alternative to the seams. My preference is the Easy Press Pen.

## Pencils

Mechanical pencils come in a variety of styles and sizes. I use 0.5 mm and 0.7 mm HB for marking on light fabric. When marking on dark fabric, I use an extrafine white chalk pencil. I prefer Bohin or Fons & Porter white chalk pencils.

## Pins

Glass or small head silk pins that are 0.4 mm or 0.5 mm in diameter and just over 1½″ long work best for precision patchwork. I rarely use pins but sometimes they are needed. *One word of caution:* Be sure to purchase heat-resistant glass head pins. Plastic head pins will melt under the heat of the iron.

## Double-Sided Tape

Use double-sided tape to hold patchwork securely to the mat when trimming small units. I prefer Sookwang brand, as it holds well and is acid-free.

## Tear-Perfect Maker Tape

Tear-Perfect Maker Tape (by C&T Publishing) is great on the back of rulers to keep them from slipping and to use as a cutting guide.

## Stickers

I use heat-resistant, residue-free, acid-free stickers, no larger than ½″ in diameter, to keep blocks organized during piecing. I prefer Trend Enterprises stickers (trendenterprises.com). Any small size, color, or pattern will work. Always test stickers before you use them!

## Lingerie Bag

For drying precuts in the dryer, see How to Prewash Fabric (page 24).

## See-Through Stabilizer

A see-through, nonwoven stabilizer is attached at the top of a Quilt Block Base. When a Quilt Block Builder is slipped under the stabilizer, the block can be seen through the stabilizer. Fabrics placed on top of the stabilizer will not slide around (see Quilt Block Bases, page 8). I prefer to use Fun-Dation (by HTC), available in 8½″ × 11″ sheets and by the yard.

## Batting

With so many different battings available on the market it can be challenging to decide which to use and why. I have narrowed my choices to three that I go back to time and time again. For a nice flat look with very little loft, I use Quilters Dream Cotton Select. For a little more loft, I use Warm and Natural (by The Warm Company). For higher loft, I prefer Hobbs Heirloom Premium 80/20 Cotton Blend.

## Plastic Storage Bins

Use clear plastic storage bins for holding notions, accessories, quilts in progress, storing strips of various sizes and yardage. I prefer clear Sterilite bins available in a variety of sizes (see Storage Bins, page 29).

# CHOOSING FABRIC

*"[This quilt] is an outburst of joy. … At the sight of it, every face brightens. How can … mere pieces of cloth sewed together have this power to lift the human spirit? No one can explain this; it is the mystery of art."*
—Rose Wilder Lane, *The Woman's Day Book of American Needlework*

## COTTON

Cotton is traditionally the fabric most quilters use in their heirloom and everyday quilts. It is a friendly fabric, has little stretch, retains its color, is long lasting, and relatively easy to work with. Cotton tends to stick to itself so there is less slippage when rotary cutting and machine piecing. Whether finger pressing or pressing with an iron, cotton is easy to press and maintains its crease. For precision patchwork, I strongly suggest purchasing only top quality, premium brands, 100% cotton fabric. Use the kind found in your local quilt store and from reputable online shops, such as the Fat Quarter Shop (fatquartershop.com).

**TIP** Testing Your Fabric

When digging deep into your stash, it may be tempting to toss in anything and everything, but keep in mind that fabrics that are loosely woven, stretchy, and of unknown fiber content will quite often make accurate piecing difficult to achieve. If there is a fabric you would like to use but are uncertain of the fiber content, try the burn test: Cut a 2″ × 2″ square of fabric and, working over a sink, burn a corner. If the fabric ignites quickly, has a yellow flame, smells a bit like paper, and leaves behind a gray or black ash, it is most likely cotton. If it melts, leaves behind plastic beads, and has a slight chemical odor, it almost certainly contains polyester—don't use it.

## COLOR

I have an emotional connection to color. Colors create a certain mood or feeling and are often the first thing I notice when shopping for fabric or viewing a quilt. Many quilters, like myself, select colors for their quilts based on intuition or a gut feeling. When auditioning fabrics if I get a twinge or feel uncomfortable, I know I need to keep working at it. Likewise, if I feel excited and my heart begins to beat faster, I know I am on the right track. My advice is to trust your heart and your instincts when making fabric selections. Along with intuition, mix in some basic knowledge of color and you will be creating beautiful, harmonious quilts with comfort and confidence in no time.

I highly recommend Joen Wolfrom's book *Color Play, Second Edition* (by C&T Publishing). It is full of information to help select fabrics for your next quilt. Her Essential Color Wheel Companion and Ultimate 3-in-1 Color Tool (both by C&T Publishing) are also valuable tools when planning a quilt in a specific color.

*Color Play: Second Edition*

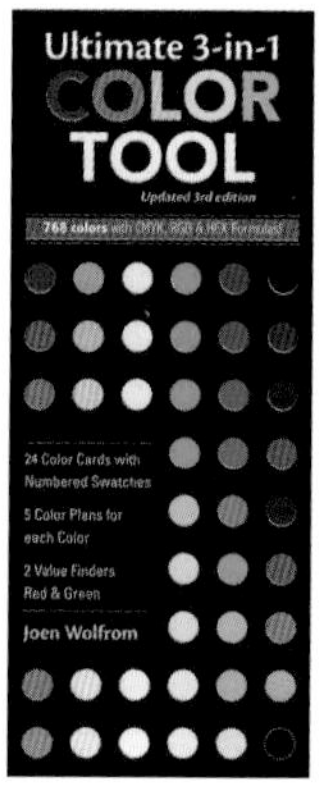


Ultimate 3-in-1 Color Tool, Updated 3rd Edition

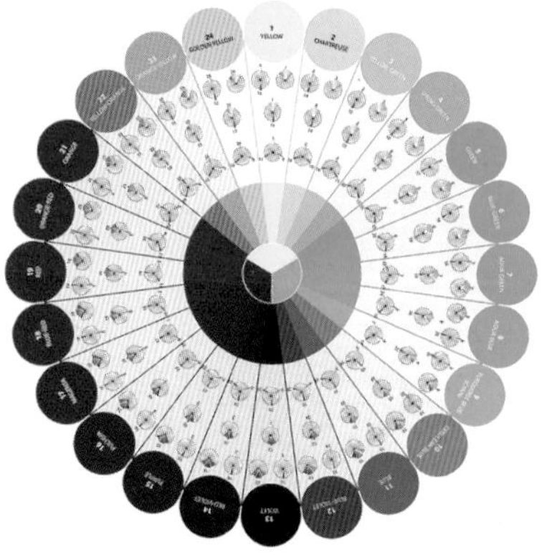

Essential Color Wheel Companion

## USING THEME PRINTS

Choosing fabrics for your next quilt can be both exciting and intimidating. As quilters, consider several factors while attempting to turn an idea into a visual form. Who is the quilt for? What is the end use? The easiest way to start is to select a theme print that conveys the feeling or style of quilt you have in mind. Then, select a background and several coordinating prints that match or blend with the theme print. Include light, medium, and dark fabrics to create contrast. Fabrics with visual texture will also add interest. To blend all the fabrics together the theme print is often used in the body of the quilt and for the borders.

Assorted print fabrics

**TIP** **Using Cues from Your Fabric**

The selvage edge of fabric usually has circles or other motifs that contain the individual colors and shades used to create that print. Use these color swatches when developing your fabric palette.

The colors on the selvage edge show the colors used to print the fabric.

## VALUE AND CONTRAST

*Value* refers to how light or dark something is. Just remember that value is relative: A fabric may appear light next to a dark color and dark when placed next to a light color.

*Contrast* refers to how similar or different things are. Creating strong contrast is necessary to see the overall pattern of the blocks in a quilt. The smaller the pieces, the more contrast is needed to maintain the overall pattern. You can create contrast using color, value, and visual texture (page 21).

You will know you have achieved good contrast between background and main print when the seam is clearly defined between the two.

**TIP** If you are not sure there is enough contrast between two or more fabrics, take a photo of them with your cell phone and convert it either to black and white or to gray scale. You will instantly see if there is enough contrast for your purposes.

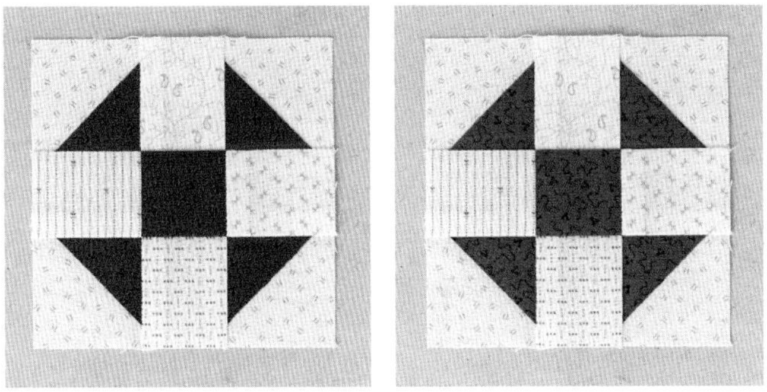

Grayscale photo shows the contrast.

### Visual Texture

Another way to add contrast is by using fabrics with various visual textures—large, medium, and small prints, dancing, directional, plaids, stripes, and polka-dot patterns. These prints add visual texture and will make your quilt more interesting.

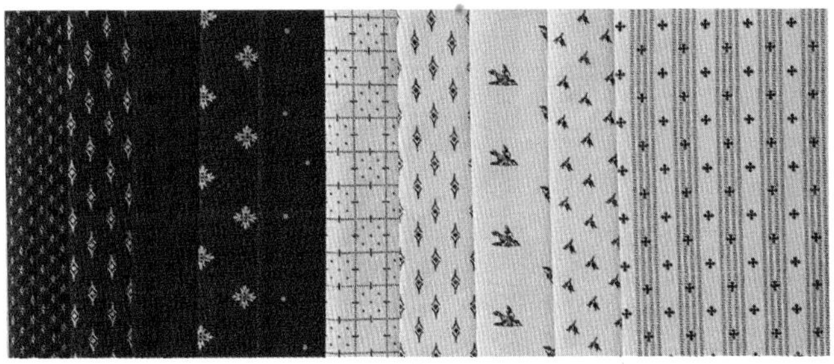

Fabrics with a variety of visual textures

## BACKGROUND FABRICS

Background fabric can be light such as white (modern), cream (heirloom), or dark such as black (Amish). The background fabric will establish the mood and style of the quilt as much as will the main prints, colors, and values.

### TIP Selecting Background Fabrics

When selecting background fabrics for heirloom style quilts, I work with fabrics that have a base of cream through beige with mini prints in single and multiple colors. A variety of tone-on-tones and prints adds interest and visual texture to the background.

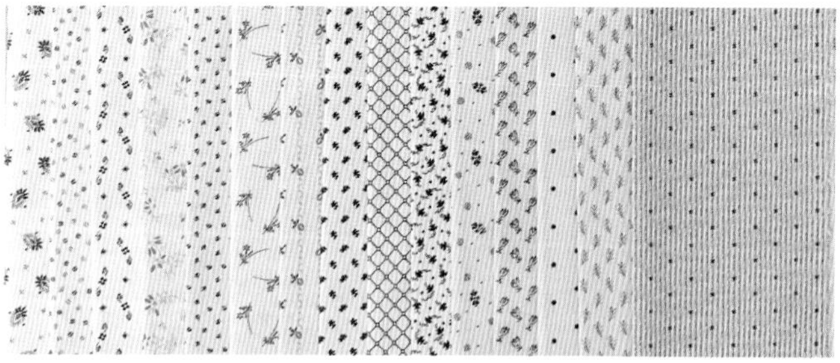

Using a variety of background fabrics adds interest.

## GUIDELINES FOR SCRAP QUILTS

While there aren't any hard and fast rules, the following are the guidelines I use to maintain good contrast when selecting fabrics for my quilts.

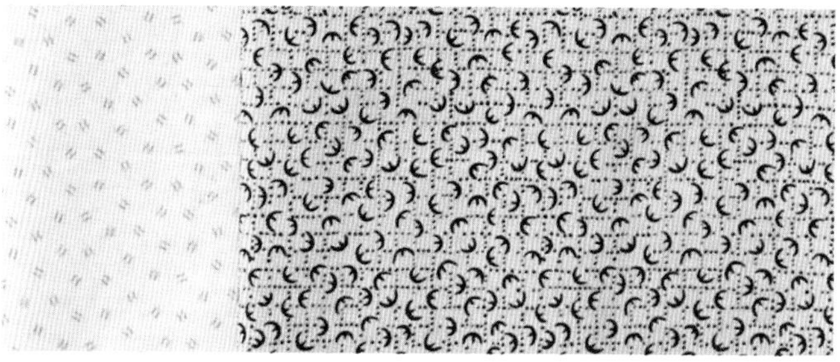

Select two background prints—one for the lightest light and the other the darkest light.

Select two main prints—one the lightest dark and the other the darkest dark.

Any print that falls within these parameters is fair game to use in your quilt. If you stray from these guidelines the quilt can appear busy and chaotic, as there is no place for the eye to rest. The design can become lost with little or no difference in value of color and contrast.

Working within these guidelines, I used more than 700 different prints in *Appleyard Lane* (page 90).

## MAINTAINING BALANCE IN CONTRAST AND DESIGN

It is difficult to predict exactly how two fabrics will work with one another until they are cut up and arranged in a block—you don't know until you sew.

A background and main print may look fabulous side by side, but once cut into smaller pieces and sewn together, the background fabric can seem busy, not provide enough contrast, or appear too dark.

Background too busy

Not enough contrast

Too dark

---

These combinations of colors, values, and visual texture may fit within the parameters of your main and background prints, but because the background prints are busy they read darker and provide less contrast with the main print. These blocks can successfully blend in with other blocks in a scrap quilt if they are not over-the-top busy in comparison to the others. They will most definitely add visual texture.

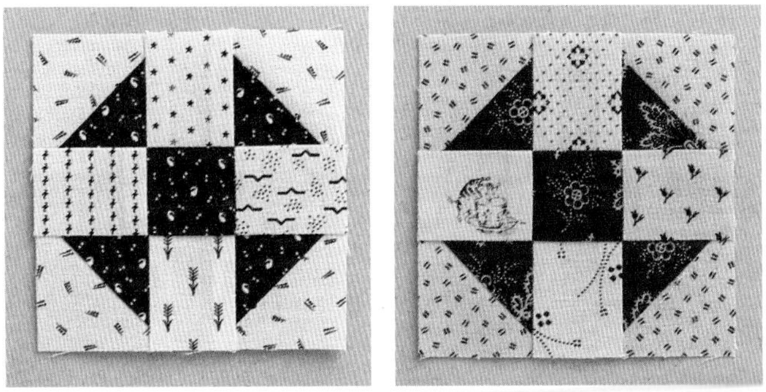

Main blends with background.

Areas of white or cream on a main print can blur the seams when they come into contact with a light background fabric. In a scrappy quilt, this scenario plays out over and over again and is actually desirable; but if you are seeking blocks with clear contrast, avoid using main prints with motifs that blend with your background fabric.

## AUDITIONING FABRIC

Auditioning fabric is the process of selecting, cutting, and arranging fabrics for a quilt or block. When auditioning fabric, if there is a print that your eye keeps going back to and gets stuck on, it is most likely too busy. Set it aside for another quilt.

**TIP** **Practice, Practice, Practice**

Put theory into practice. The more you work with your fabrics the more comfortable and confident you will become.

## STASH BUILDING

The number of fabrics in your quilts will vary depending on your stash. How uniform or random a scrap quilt appears depends on the placement of lights, mediums, and darks within the quilt regardless of the number of different fabrics used.

### Specialty Cut Bundles

A great way to choose fabrics and quickly grow your stash is to purchase specialty cut bundles, also called *precuts*. Many manufacturers offer precut bundles that are made up of one of each print in a collection. Precuts are available in several different sizes and shapes. Fabric designers often include in their collections a theme print, background, lights, mediums, darks, and fabrics with visual texture.

Precut bundles

**TIP** **Shopping for Precuts**

My favorite online shop for precuts is the Fat Quarter Shop (fatquartershop.com).

*Best Precuts for the Easy Precision Piecing System*

**Precut strip bundles:** 40 strips 2½″ × 42″

**Precut square packs:** 42 squares 10″ × 10″

**Jumbo precut strip bundles:** 20 strips 5″ × 44″

**Fat eighth bundles:** 9″ × 21″

**Fat quarter bundles:** 18″ × 21″

I love buying precuts because I can get the whole line all at once. I prefer to purchase fat quarter bundles, but if a collection is not available in fat quarters, I will purchase smaller precuts in sizes suitable for the Easy Precision Piecing System.

**TIP** Sharing Goodies

If you have a friend who shares your taste in fabrics, purchase several different fat quarter bundles and split them.

When making scrap quilts, a fat eighth goes a long way. My local quilt shop offers ten fat eighths bundled in groups of colors. These little bundles are perfect for stash building.

## Off the Bolt

When shopping for stash building online, at my local quilt shop, or while traveling, I usually purchase ¼ yard for patchwork and accents, ½ yard if I really like the fabric, and 1 yard if I absolutely love it. When purchasing fabric for a specific quilt, I will buy the amounts recommended in the pattern; and if I really love the fabric and intend to use it in other quilts, I purchase an extra ¼ yard to add to my stash.

# PREPARING FABRIC

*If you are an experienced quiltmaker and are tempted to skip this chapter, please don't. Proper preparation helps ensure precision, which is what this book is all about.*

## PREWASHING

Although the choice is up to you how to prepare your fabrics, I choose to prewash all my cotton fabrics before they ever get into my quilts. I wash them either by hand or machine and then dry them in the dryer. Washing fabrics aids in the removal of chemicals, pesticides, and excess dyes. Drying in the dryer helps prevent further shrinkage.

If not prewashed, chemicals used to keep cottons pest free may remain on the fabric and can be released into the air you breathe and onto your hands when pressing and handling.

To prevent further shrinkage, always dry fabrics in the dryer. Pressed and air-dried fabric will continue to shrink under the heat of the iron and when the quilt is washed. This will cause fabrics to pucker and the quilt will not lie flat.

I learned the importance of machine drying fabric the hard way. I was working on a project with a deadline looming before me and ran out of fabric. I purchased more and decided to save time by washing the fabric in the sink. Then, I rolled it in a towel and pressed it dry. I started cutting, piecing, and pressing, and all seemed fine until I went to add the new blocks to the machine dried blocks. To my dismay the new blocks were ¼″ smaller than the others! I lost a lot of time. I had to machine wash and dry my fabrics and start all over again. I did get the project done on time but it was a lesson I will never forget.

After washing and drying fabric, test dark fabrics for color fastness. Place a 2″ square of the piece you want to test on top of a white piece of cotton fabric. Wet it and let it sit for a few minutes, and then press it with an iron to see if any more color comes out. If the fabric is still bleeding, use a color fixative such as Retayne (by G&K Craft Industries) and follow the instruction on the packaging. Test for color fastness once again. If the fabric is still bleeding, do not use it in your quilt. This is especially important when working with reds and blues, as they tend to bleed more than others.

### How to Prewash Fabric

With all prewashing, whether by hand or machine, separate lights from darks. Use cold water with a mild detergent, allowing the detergent to dissolve or disperse in the water before adding fabrics—detergent, whether powder or liquid, placed directly on fabrics may stain the fabrics.

**TIP** No Wringing!

After washing, do not wring the water out of the fabrics, as this will cause unwanted wrinkles and creases.

#### *Precut Strip Bundles and Precut Square Packs*

These smaller precuts are best hand washed.

**1.** Fill a sink or bucket with cold water and a small amount of mild detergent.

**2.** Place the fabrics in the water one at a time, pressing them down to ensure they are saturated.

**3.** Allow the fabrics to soak for about 30 minutes.

**4.** Drain and gently press the water out of the fabrics.

**5.** Gently, taking care not to stretch the fabrics, place them flat on a towel.

**6.** Roll up the towel and give it a gentle squeeze to help remove the excess water.

**7.** Put the fabrics into a lingerie bag, place it in the dryer, and dry until just dry.

**8.** Remove the fabrics from the lingerie bag, trim frayed edges, and lay flat.

#### *Fat Eighths, Fat Quarters, and Yardage*

These larger precuts and yardage are best washed on a delicate cycle in cold water.

**1.** Select the setting that most resembles the size of load you are putting in the washing machine.

**2.** For front-loading machines, follow the instructions provided by the manufacturer. For top-loaders, begin filling the machine with water; add a small amount of mild detergent and allow it to dissolve.

**3.** Open the fabrics and place them in the machine one piece at a time and allow them to go through the entire wash cycle.

**4.** Remove the fabrics from the washing machine one piece at a time.

**5.** Untwist, trim the frayed threads to no longer than 1″, and place the fabrics in the dryer.

**6.** Dry on a delicate setting.

**7.** Once the fabrics are just dry, remove them from the dryer and lay flat.

**TIP** When drying fabric, check them after about 15 minutes in the dryer to see how dry they are. If they're still damp, continue drying and check again in 5 minutes. Do not over-dry, as wrinkles and creases will set into the fibers and be extremely difficult to remove.

**PRECISION PIECING KEY:**

## Fabric Prep Is the First Step in Precision Piecing

Stable fabric is key to precise cutting—a prerequisite for precise piecing. Using a starch alternative and pressing adds body to the fabric and stabilizes it so there is less stretching, which results in more accurate rotary cutting and piecing. To avoid stretching fabric dampened with a starch alternative, use a light touch with the iron.

## STARCHING AND PRESSING

I prefer to use Easy Press Fabric Treatment (page 17) to add body to fabric after washing and drying. I am sensitive to scents and love the fact that Easy Press is unscented.

*Note:* I recommend cutting fabric into manageable sizes for starching and pressing. For suggested sizes, see Cutting and Folding for Starching and Storage (page 28).

**TIP** **Why Using Corn-Based Starch Is a Bad Idea**

I live deep in the country, and just as I do not feed birds seeds that undesirable critters may be interested in, I do not serve up a batch of corn-based starched fabrics to bugs such as silverfish. Silverfish eat natural fibers, such as cotton, and love cornstarch. A starch alternative may be a little more expensive than homemade and some regular corn-based starches on the market, but I prefer to spend a bit more money and enjoy the peace of mind.

## Layering for Starching and Pressing

*Note:* If you have the option on the nozzle of the starch alternative for either spray or stream, select spray.

**1.** Separate the lights from darks, and stack the fabrics right side up on your pressing surface.

Stack fabric for starching and pressing.

**2.** Working with one stack, take the top fabric off the stack and place it parallel to the other fabrics.

Start with the top piece of fabric.

Slightly overlap the top edge of the fabric piece about ⅛″. This way your ironing surface will not get soaked with the starch alternative along the top edge of the fabric between the two stacks.

**3.** Hold the spray bottle about 8″ from the fabric and liberally spray with starch alternative so the surface is mostly covered but not soaked. You will notice that the fabric draws in once sprayed, but do not worry.

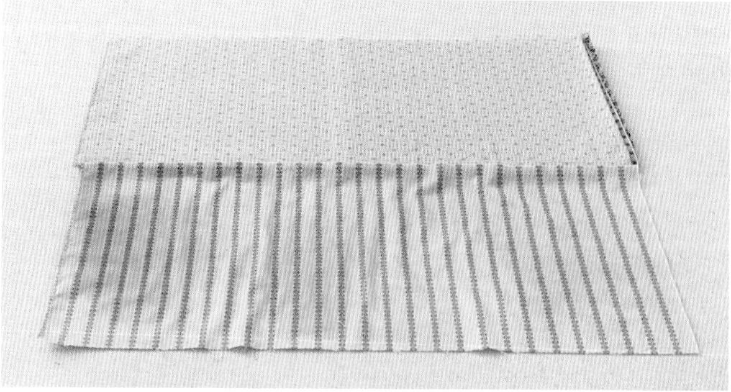

Sprayed fabric draws in.

**4.** Take the next piece off the stack and center it on top of the piece just sprayed.

**5.** Place your hands together in the center, palms down, using a patting motion and working with the left hand to the left and right hand to the right, gently pat the fabric from the center to the edges smoothing out the fabric below.

**6.** After the fabric is smooth, spray the top piece.

**7.** Repeat Steps 3–6 until all the fabrics are sprayed.

**8.** Turn the stack over so they are now wrong side up. Pat again from the center to the edges, so the fabrics are nice and flat.

*Remember:* The pursuit of quality takes a little more time; however, the results are well worth the effort.

## Pressing Damp Fabric

Press with a dry iron on cotton setting. No steam. (See Precision Piecing Key: Use a Dry Iron, page 13.)

**1.** Place the iron on the top fabric in the top right corner, let it sit in one place for about 3 seconds, pick the iron up and move to the next spot, slightly overlapping the previous. Set it in the new place for about 3 seconds, move to the next spot, and so on. Work from the top right corner toward the bottom, then back to the top from right to left, then left to right, repeating until the top fabric is dry.

Pressing damp fabric

**2.** Test for dryness with your opposite hand. After the fabric is completely dry, begin to *gently and slowly* slide the iron up and down from right to left. This motion will remove any impressions left on the fabric from the iron.

**3.** After the top fabric is dry and impressions removed, peel the fabric from the stack and set it aside on a flat surface.

**4.** Begin pressing the next fabric, repeating Steps 1–3. Continue in this manner until the entire stack is starched and pressed.

While fabric is damp, the iron must be picked up and set down. Do not slide the iron on the fabric when it is wet, as this will cause stretching and distortion. The heat from the iron penetrates through the top layer to the fabric below; thus, when the top fabric is dry and removed, the next fabric is already drying, making it easier to press

- Stacking and starching gives the product time to soak through and bond with the fibers, resulting in a nice crisp press that only needs to be done once.
- When starching one fabric at a time, spray the right side of the fabric. Turn the fabric wrong side up. Wait about 15 seconds before starting to press. This will give the starch time to soak through the fabric and result in a nicer press.

If you notice burn marks on your fabric, lower the heat on your iron.

**TIP** **Starching Yardage**

Liberally spray the entire surface of the fabric. Hang to dry, then add a light spray of starch alternative and press.

## STORING YOUR STASH

I have been quilting for just over 27 years and have accumulated a delightful stash of fabrics. To enhance efficiency, I organize my fabrics by theme, color, lights, and darks.

**TIP** **Maintaining a Stash**

Part of my stash is made up of fabrics that I have purchased over the years or swapped with friends, which means that I have very little left of some of my old favorites. While it is hard to say goodbye, I have come to the conclusion that these old fabrics want to be in a quilt, not hanging out in a bin. When I gather the nerve to cut up the last bit of one of these old friends, I glue a snippet into a "No more of this fabric left" swatch book. This way if I go looking for a certain fabric and it is there in the swatch book, I know to look no further. Fingers crossed I wasn't looking for it because I made a mistake!

### Cutting and Folding for Starching and Storage

*Fat Eighths*

I cut all fabrics intended for scrappy quilts into approximately 9″ × 21″ pieces, the size of a fat eighth. I have found that this size is easy to starch, press, subcut into strips, and store.

*Note:* I don't cut entire yardage into fat eighths, I cut 1 strip 9″ × 42″ then subcut into 2 strips 9″ × 21″.

I fold the extra 9″ × 21″ strips over an Omnigrid 4″ × 14″ or 4″ × 8″ ruler for easy storage. Larger pieces are folded and stored in extra-large bins until ready to be cut and prepared.

**1.** Fold the fabric in half, raw edge to selvage.

**2.** Center the ruler on top.

Center the ruler.

**3.** Fold the fabric over the ruler and pull the ruler out through the bottom.

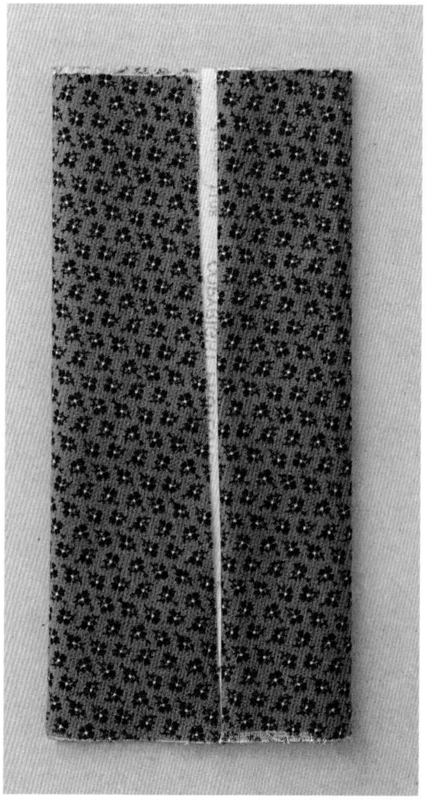

Fold the fabric.

**4.** Turn the fabric horizontally and center the ruler on top.

Turn the fabric and center the ruler.

**5.** Fold the fabric over the ruler, pull the ruler out through the bottom and store.

*Fat Quarters and ¼ Yard Off the Bolt*

**1.** Fold the selvages parallel for fat quarters and selvage to selvage for off the bolt.

*Note:* Fabric is folded correctly if it is 9″ × 21″, incorrectly if 10½″ × 18″.

**2.** Trim the frayed edges.

**3.** Cut along the fold.

**4.** Place the two pieces in separate stacks: one to be further prepared for piecing, the other in a stack for folding and storage.

## Storage Bins

I use clear storage bins to keep my stash organized whether stacked, folded, or in strips. They come in several different sizes, are sturdy with latches that securely lock into place, and are stackable. I prefer to use Sterilite bins. I have found the most useful sizes are (measurements are length × width × height):

- Medium Clip Box (11″ × 6⅝″ × 5⅜″)
- Large Clip Box (14″ × 11″ × 3¼″)
- Deep Clip Box (14″ × 11″ × 6¼″)
- 28-Quart Storage Box (23 × 16¼″ × 6″)

I use medium bins to store folded fat quarters and fat eighths.

I use large bins to organize strips. They are labeled and stacked according to the size of the strips. I store dark and light strips in separate bins.

The large and deep bins hold standard 8½″ × 11″ notes and books, making them the perfect bins for storing work in progress and great for toting to classes and retreats.

Yardage is sorted into themes and then folded, stacked by color, and stored in extra-large (28-quart) bins.

I also store prepared fabrics stacked flat by color and theme in extra-large (28-quart) bins. I prefer to keep my fabrics nicely stacked and sorted by color after starching, pressing, and cutting. This way when I need more fabric, I don't waste time starching and pressing again. Sorting by color means I can easily find the fabric I need.

My current project is organized and portable in Sterilite's Stack and Carry 2-Layer Handle Box (14⅜ × 10¾″ × 7⅝″). These stackable bins easily accommodate notes, patterns, books, Quilt Block Bases (page 8), blocks, and fabrics. Each layer can be removed for quick access to the items inside. I love these whether working on my project at home, classes, or retreats.

Stack and Carry 2-Layer Handle Box

For larger blocks and their Quilt Block Builders (page 7), an IRIS Scrapbook Chest (available at craft and hobby stores) that holds scrapbook cases can easily hold Quilt Block Builders and blocks up to 14″ × 14″. I store all my oversize blocks and Quilt Block Builders in these cases.

Scrapbook case for larger blocks

# PRECISION CUTTING

## KNOW YOUR FABRIC

For successful rotary cutting and machine piecing, it is important to understand the characteristics of cotton fabric and the terms used to describe them.

**Selvages** are the finished edges of the fabric and are created during the weaving process. These edges are thicker and more densely woven than the rest of the fabric. You will often find important information printed on the selvage, such as the company, designer, and even the colors used to create the print. Due to the thicker properties of the selvages, they can interfere with precision piecing, so when subcutting, cut them off and set them aside or throw them away.

**Grain** refers to the lengthwise and crosswise threads, both of which are considered straight of grain in rotary cutting and patchwork.

**Lengthwise** threads, also known as *warp*, run parallel to the selvage along the length of the fabric and have the least amount of stretch—quiltmakers often suggest cutting borders along the lengthwise grain to take advantage of this.

**Crosswise** threads, also known as *weft*, run perpendicular to the selvage and have very little stretch. Also known as the width of the fabric, most rotary cutting is done along the crosswise grain.

### TIP Checking for Lengthwise or Crosswise Grain

After fabric has been cut into squares, if you are unsure which is crosswise or lengthwise grain, hold the fabric between your thumb and index finger of both hands and give it a little snap—the lengthwise grain will have a strong snapping sound and the crosswise grain will have a dull thudding sound.

**True bias** runs at a 45° angle to the lengthwise and crosswise grains and has a significant amount of stretch.

- When fussy cutting or cutting diamonds, hexagons, and irregular shapes, the bias can end up along the edge of a block. To keep bias from stretching, gently apply a starch alternative (page 46) along the cut edges and press to dry.
- To take advantage of its stretching properties, the bias is often used for narrow segments or stems when appliquéing and binding scalloped or other round edges of quilts and place mats.

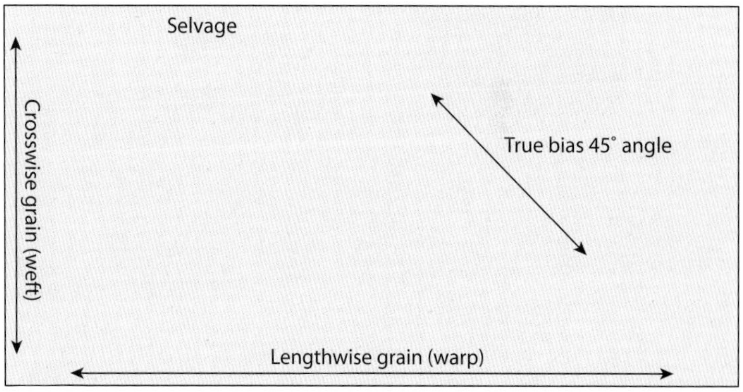


### TIP Watch Out for Bias Edges

For best piecing results when rotary cutting, keep the straight of grain along the outside edges of blocks and the bias on the inside. Blocks with bias on the outside edges can stretch, warp, and lose their shape. Blocks with straight of grain on the outside edges are easier to work with, will lie flat, and easily retain their shape.

# BEGINNERS GUIDE TO ROTARY CUTTING

Always use prepared fabrics when precision cutting (see Preparing Fabric, page 24).

## Unfinished and Finished Sizes

Strips, squares, triangles, and other shapes for patchwork use ¼″ seam allowances. All the step-by-step instructions and patterns in this book include the ¼″ seam allowance in the cutting instructions.

**Finished** refers to the size of the piece once sewn into a block.

**Unfinished** refers to the size of the piece and includes the seam allowances.

The red square is the finished size; the frame surrounding it is the ¼″ seam allowance added to all four sides.

## Holding the Rotary Cutter

Rotary cutters are created for comfort. When used correctly you can comfortably cut for hours without causing damage to your wrist.

**1.** Place your hands at your sides. Look down and see how your thumb and forefinger naturally form a U shape.

**2.** Pick up the cutter and rest the handle in the palm of your hand. Place your index finger on the grooved ridge along the side, resting the tip of your finger in the curve. Place your thumb on the front of the handle and wrap the rest of your fingers around the back of the handle. You are holding the cutter properly if you will still see the U formed by your thumb and index finger.

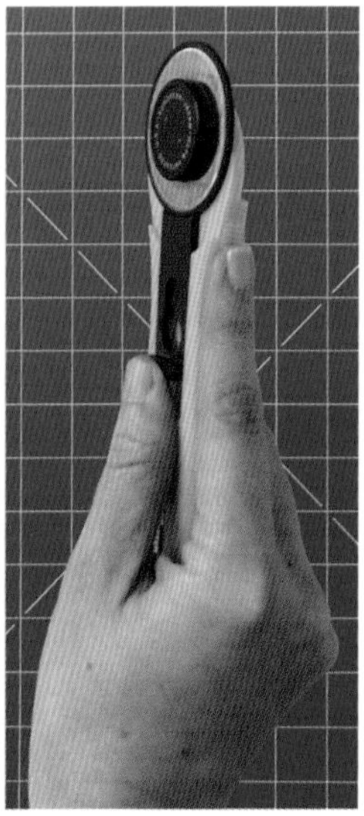

Proper way to hold a rotary cutter

**3.** Use your thumb to pull down on the safety cover to expose the blade when cutting and to push it back in safety position when not in use.

## Hints and Tips for Prolonging Blade Life

- Due to the extra pressure you must exert to cleanly cut through fabric, a dull blade is more dangerous than a sharp blade. Also, a dull blade can cut deep wide grooves in your mat that will not heal. Keep new blades on hand so when one gets dull you can replace it right away. Keep your old dull blades to cut paper and plastic.
- New blades come with a thin layer of oil on them. This helps to lubricate the cutter and allows the blade to roll smoothly.
- Each time you replace the blade, wipe away lint from the cutter, safety cover, and tension disc.
- Keep the tension screw at the back snug so the blade does not wobble when cutting.
- Always make sure your cutting surface is free of pins or other items that could damage the blade.

## For the Sake of Safety

I have been teaching precision rotary cutting for more than 25 years. I have seen a lot of accidents occur due to improper use of the cutter and have unfortunately had to take students to the hospital on two occasions for stitches. The following tips are from experience at home and in the classroom. Please be careful, always pay attention to each and every cut, and respect the sharpness of the blade.

- Keep fingers away from the edge of the ruler you are cutting along, as it is easy to accidently cut your finger if it strays off the edge.
- Always close/sheath the blade after each cut. If an open blade is set on the table and gets under fabrics it is easy to cut yourself or a classmate when shifting things about.
- Wear shoes that cover the top of your feet when cutting. A rotary cutter can easily fall from the table and land blade down on top of your foot.
- Never talk with an open blade in your hand, waving your arms about, as it is very easy to forget that the blade is open, and a cut can occur before you ever know what has happened.
- Lastly when at home, keep rotary cutters up high when not in use so curious children cannot reach them.

## PREPARING FOR THE FIRST CUT

- Long strips are most often cut across the crosswise grain then subcut into shapes.
- To ensure accurate cuts, cut a maximum of two layers at a time.
- If you are new to rotary cutting, practice cutting on a ½ yard of fabric that you do not mind making cutting mistakes on. This will help reduce the stress of miscuts if they happen.

### Folding the Fabric on Grain

Due to washing or the way the fabric was rolled on the bolt, the fabric may not be folded on grain. Use the following procedure to fold the fabric properly so you can even the edges.

**1.** Fold fabric wrong sides together, selvage to selvage.

**2.** Using both hands, pick up the fabric holding onto the selvages with a hand at each corner. Place your thumb in front, middle finger on the back, and index finger between the two layers. Holding the fabric this way you can easily shift the front fabric along your index fingers using your thumbs. The back fabric will remain stationary.

**3.** Look at the bottom folded edge. If it is wonky shift the fabric with your thumbs along your index fingers until it is hanging straight. The straight grains are now lined up and fabric is ready for cutting.

**4.** Place the fabric on your cutting mat with the selvages away from you and the fold closest to you. You are now ready to make the first cut, evening up the edges.

**TIP** If you see a V at the fold after you have cut a strip, the fabric was not folded on grain before cutting. To avoid this common cutting problem, be sure to fold the fabric properly on grain.

Line up grainlines.

## SQUARING UP YARDAGE

I use the two-ruler method to square up the edges of my fabric. This method is guaranteed to produce an accurate straight edge. You will need a 6″ × 24″ and 6″ × 12″ ruler or equivalent, a rotary cutter, and an 18″ × 24″ self-healing mat.

**1.** Align a horizontal line on the 6″ × 12″ ruler with the bottom fold of the fabric.

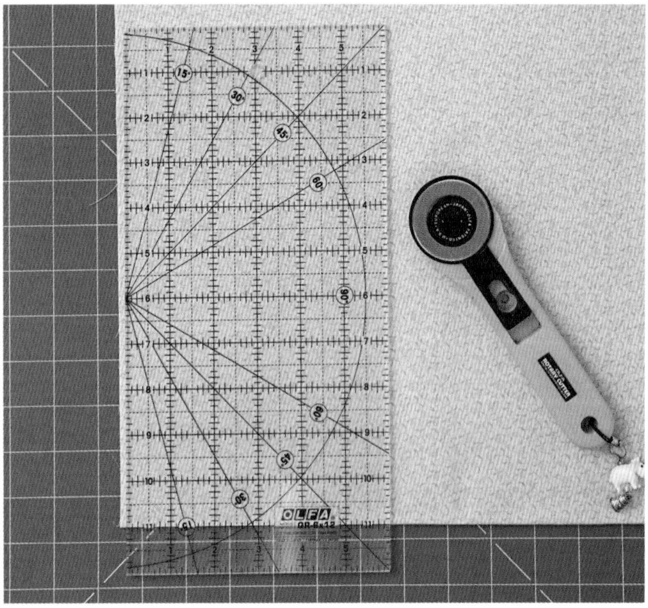


Align ruler.

**2.** Butt a 6″ × 24″ ruler to the left, up to and against the 6″ × 12″ ruler covering the fabric that needs to be trimmed away plus about ⅛″.

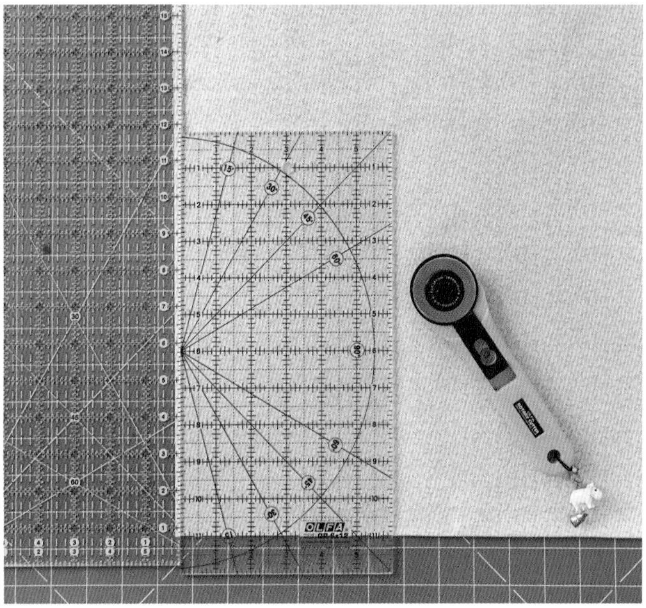


Butt a second ruler up against the first ruler.

**3.** Remove the 6″ × 12″ ruler. You will be cutting along the right-hand side of the 6″ × 24″ ruler.

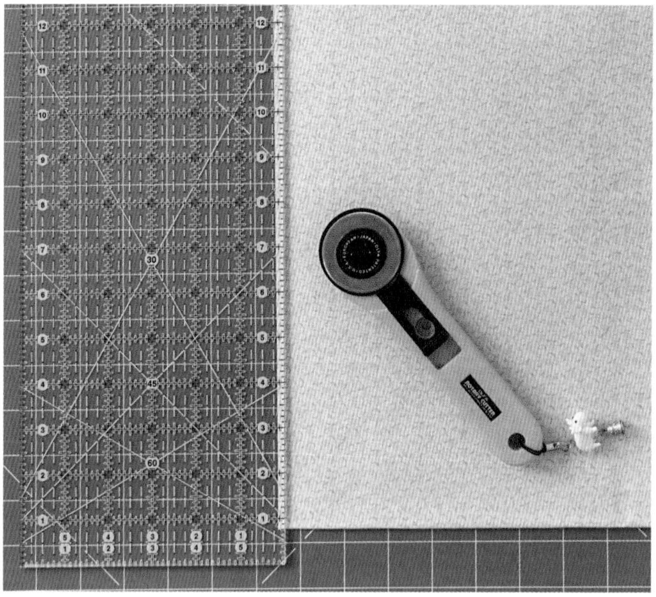

Remove the first ruler.

**4.** Hold the long ruler down with the left hand, spreading out your thumb and fingers, and place your pinkie finger off the ruler on the left edge. This finger serves as an anchor and helps keep the ruler from moving as you are cutting.

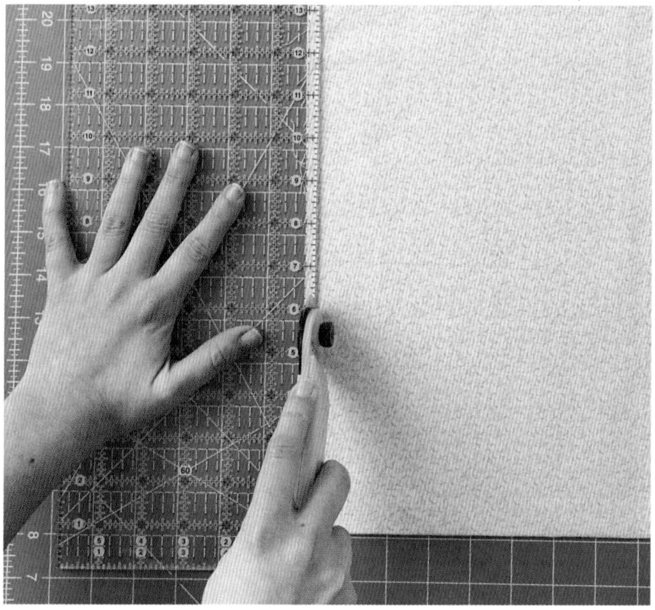

Hold the ruler firmly while cutting.

**5.** Start your cut about ¼″ before the fold. Begin rolling the cutter pressing down on the mat with the blade at a slight angle up to and against the bottom edge of the ruler. When the cutter and the fingertips of your left hand are parallel, stop rolling the cutter, but do not pick it up. Walk your left hand vertically up the ruler, placing your thumb where your fingertips are and spreading your fingertips up toward the top of the ruler, and place your pinkie just off the left edge once again.

**6.** Begin rolling the cutter, pausing when you reach the fingertips of your left hand. Continue to walk and roll to the top of the fabric up to and through the selvage.

**7.** After cutting, before removing the ruler, gently slide the bigger piece of fabric to the right to make sure you have cut cleanly through both layers of fabric.

## PRACTICE CUTTING

When cutting always take care and time when measuring before making a cut. Just as true for quiltmaking as for carpentry: Measure twice, cut once. For practice, cut 2″-wide strips.

After you have squared up the fabric, move the ruler over so the vertical 2″ line is fully on the cut edge of the fabric.

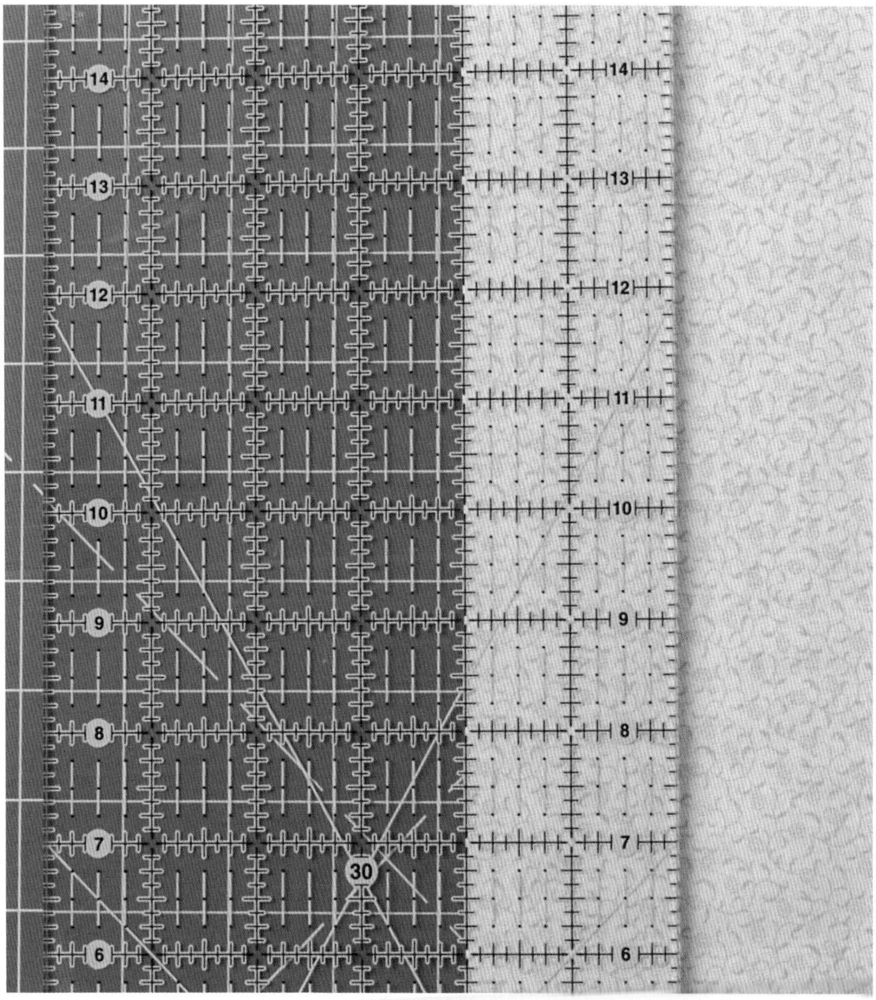


Make sure vertical line is fully on the edge of the fabric.

## QUICK REFERENCE FOR PRECISION CUTTING

*If you are left-handed, reverse the cutting instructions.*

- Press the cutter up to and against the ruler at a slight angle toward the bottom edge of the ruler for a more accurate cut.
- To help stabilize the ruler, keep the cutter and your left hand parallel during the cut.
- Always stand to cut. Being above your work will provide you with a better view, more control over your cuts, and improved accuracy.
- Make sure you keep the ruler accurately aligned on the fabric as you walk your hand up the ruler.
- If you are having difficulty because the ruler is slipping, apply a strip of Tear-Perfect Maker Tape (page 17) to the back of the ruler. You can still see the markings and the ruler will be less likely to slip.
- Roll the cutter away from you, except when trimming four-patches and half-square triangles (page 58).
- Use firm, even, continuous pressure while cutting.
- Avoid rolling the blade back and forth in a chopping motion.
- Change the blade if it is skipping or you are having to apply more pressure to get through both layers.

**PRECISION PIECING KEY:**

## Careful Cutting

It's important to make sure the 2″ line of the ruler is fully on the fabric when you cut, so the piece is large enough to compensate for the width of the thread and the ¼″ seam when you are piecing (page 35).

1. Line up a horizontal line exactly along the fold. Make the cut.

2. Move the fabric away from the ruler to the right to make sure you have cut cleanly through both layers.

3. Continue practicing making 2″ cuts until you are comfortable. The more you practice cutting the more comfortable and confident you will become.

If you are no longer able to match both the horizontal line of the ruler exactly along the fold and the vertical line of the ruler exactly along the cut edge, you will need to square up the cut edge as you did when you made the first cut (see Squaring Up Yardage, page 34). You will usually need to square up after about three cuts

## SQUARING UP SMALL CUTS OF NONDIRECTIONAL FABRIC

When working with small pieces of fabric, such as fat eighths, cut through one layer at a time along the lengthwise grain.

**1.** Fold the fabric wrong sides together, lining up the grainlines, and cut edge to selvage, extending the cut edge 1″ beyond the edge of the selvage (see Folding Fabric on Grain, page 33).

**2.** Hold the fabric in the corners with both hands and look at the fold. If it is wonky, move the front fabric until the fold is straight.

**3.** Place fabric selvage down, folded edge to the right and cut edge to the left, on the cutting mat.

**4.** Place one ruler vertically along the cut edge, covering the uneven edge plus approximately ⅛″ (see Squaring Up Yardage, page 34).

**5.** Place the second ruler horizontally on the fabric, lining up a vertical line exactly with the fold.

**6.** Butt up the two rulers next to each other, keeping the second ruler squared up exactly along the fold.

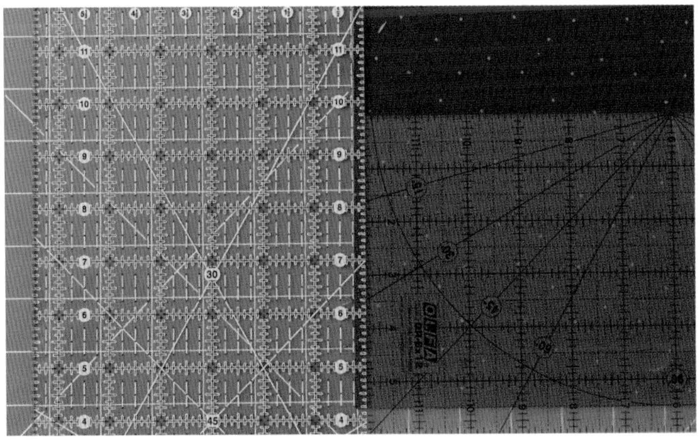

Fold the cut edge 1″ beyond the selvage edge.

**7.** Remove the horizontal ruler and make the cut.

**8.** Open the fabric and cut through one layer, measuring from the squared edge.

**TIP** Fussy Cutting Directional Fabric

- When cutting directional fabric, do not square up the fabric; instead, use the pattern of the print to determine where to cut.
- Prints with stripes, vines, and directional motifs can be fussy cut into strips and subcut into squares, particularly if there is an area on that fabric that you would like to focus on or spotlight within your blocks.

**1.** Look at the print and determine how you would like it to appear on the strip or within the block.

**2.** To cut 1½″ strips, place the first ruler on top of the fabric, with the stripe or motif centered under the ¾″ line.

**3.** Butt up the second ruler to the left.

**4.** Remove the first ruler and cut along the right edge of the remaining ruler.

**5.** Move the ruler so the 1½″ line is now fully on top of the edge of the fabric, with the print or motif centered under the ¾″ line, and make the cut.

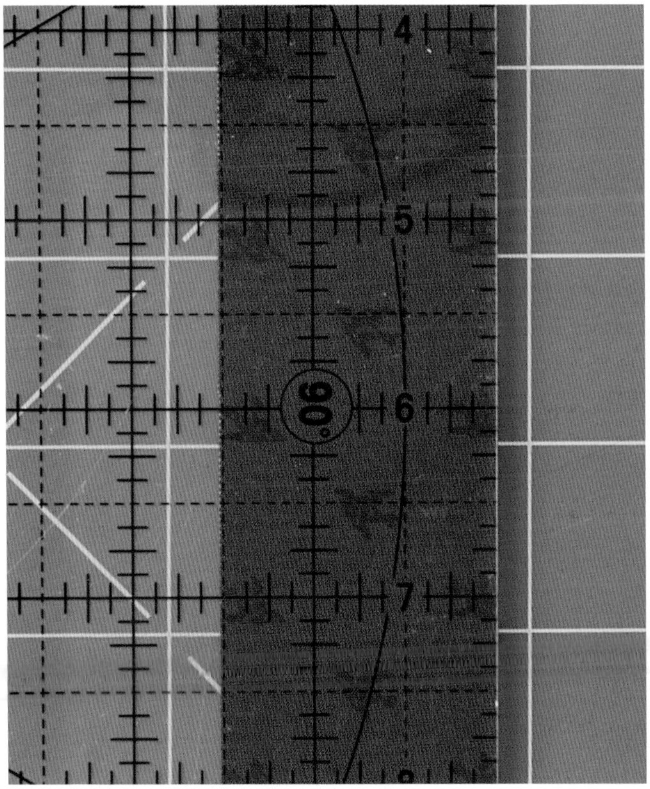

Proper placement of ruler for fussy cutting directional fabric

Use the same techniques when cutting wider or narrower strips, keeping the motif centered in the middle of the strip or square. When subcutting squares, center the motif in the middle of the cut.

# *the* PRECISE PATCHWORK SEAM

A sewing machine is an extremely valuable tool. The more knowledge you have about your sewing machine, the better your stitch quality, the more improved your accuracy, and the more professional your finished product will be.

**PRECISION PIECING KEY:**

## Maintaining a Balanced Straight Stitch

The stitches are the foundation of patchwork; they hold the quilt together. A good balanced straight stitch is essential for precision piecing. When a seam is pressed, the fabric is molded to the path the thread has taken. If the stitches are too long and loose, the thread will show at the seam and the patchwork can come apart. If the stitches are too short and tight, the fabric will draw together and pucker, resulting in patches that are too small. If the path of the thread is loose, crooked, and wonky, the seams will be loose, crooked, and wonky. If the path of the thread is balanced, straight, and accurate, the seams will be balanced, straight, and accurate.

**TIP** A great reference tool for understanding and taking care of your sewing machine is *You and Your Sewing Machine* by Bernie Tobisch (from C&T Publishing).

## SEWING MACHINE BASICS FOR BEGINNERS

Get to know your machine. Skills such as adjusting tension, stitch length, and needle position are fundamental to the quality of a precise patchwork seam. If you do not know how to adjust these, consult your manual or contact your local dealer for help.

### Adjusting the Tension for Precise Sewing

- Set the upper tension to normal and make adjustments from there. Consult your manual to find what the normal setting is on your particular machine.

*Note: Wood and cord props are used below to show tension*

- A balanced stitch will have threads interlocked midway between the two layers of fabric, with no loops on the top or bottom of the seam and no puckers in the fabric.

Balanced tension

*Continued on next page*

- If the bobbin thread shows on the top side of the seam and the top thread is straight, the upper tension is tighter than the lower.
- If top thread loops show on the underside of the seam and the lower thread is straight, the upper tension is looser than the lower.

Upper tension too tight

Upper tension too loose

- If the thread is straight either on the top or on the bottom, the stitches can easily be pulled out.
- Assume the lower tension to be correct and make adjustments to the upper tension as much as possible.

### *Tension Tip*

To raise the knot, raise the (top) tension to lower the knot lower the (top) tension.

- If there is no change after adjusting the upper tension, check to see if there is lint caught between the tension discs or between the spring of the bobbin case.
- Bobbin tension should be adjusted only if the problem cannot be corrected by adjusting the upper tension or with the removal of lint. If you find you need to adjust the bobbin tension, mark a dot on the bobbin case where the tension screw is before you begin turning it. Turn small increments at a time. Think of the hands of a clock and turn only the space of 5-minute increments. Check results then adjust again if necessary. Remember this simple and fun adage, "Lefty loosey, righty tighty." If you want the bobbin tension to be looser, turn the screw to the left (counterclockwise). For tighter tension, turn to the right (clockwise). Keep making small adjustments until you are satisfied with the quality of the stitches. For more help with adjusting your bobbin case, consult your manual or check with your local sewing machine technician.

## Winding a Uniform Bobbin

A uniformly wound bobbin is essential for precise patchwork. A loosely wound bobbin can result in uneven stitches. An overfull bobbin will not turn smoothly in the bobbin case. The thread needs to be wound on the bobbin evenly, snug and not overfilled. If you don't know how to wind a uniform bobbin, consult your manual.

## Quick Guide to Threading Your Sewing Machine

- *Make sure the presser foot is up at all times when threading your machine.* This will keep the tension discs separated while you are threading, and the thread will lie in the correct position between the tension discs for sewing. If the machine is threaded with the presser foot down, chances are the thread is not between the tension discs, which will result in upper thread loops on the bottom of your work. To check that the thread is in the upper discs after the machine is threaded (including through the eye of the needle), lower the presser foot and pull on the upper thread as it comes through the eye of the needle toward the back of the machine. If you feel resistance and the needle is slightly bending toward the back of your machine, then you know the thread is in the tension discs; if there is no resistance, it is possible that the thread is not between the discs or lint is trapped between them.
- Whenever possible use a vertical spool pin. This allows the spool to turn when stitching and to feed the thread properly while sewing. When using a horizontal spool pin, the thread tends to twist coming off the spool and can produce crooked, uneven stitches in your work.
- If the spool of thread you are using has stickers on the top and/or bottom of the spool, remove them. The adhesive can transfer to the spool pin, build up over time, and stick onto and hold the spool of thread. This will keep the spool from turning properly, thus resulting in uneven stitches or, even worse, a broken thread.

## STITCH LENGTH FOR PRECISION PIECING

Set the stitch length to 1.8–2.0 mm or 12–14 stitches per inch. This shorter stitch will not come undone at the edges when subcutting and pressing, there will be no gaps between stitches, and a seam ripper can fit under them.

### Test Your Stitch

*Note:* When testing stitch quality, always use the same thread and fabric you are using in your quilt.

1. Place the ¼″ patchwork foot and straight stitch plate, if you have one, on your machine

2. Raise the presser foot.

3. If your sewing machine comes with one, place the thread onto the vertical spool pin and thread as usual.

4. Set the upper tension to normal.

5. Wind a bobbin with the same thread you are using on the top. Thread the bobbin case and bring the bobbin thread up through the stitch plate.

6. Cut a piece of scrap fabric about 5″ × 4″. Fold the fabric in half lengthwise, right sides together.

7. Set the stitch length to 1.8–2.0 mm or 12–14 stitches per inch.

8. Sew through the center of the fabric from top to bottom. Trim the threads and remove the fabric from machine.

9. Look at the stitches. If you are not satisfied with the quality, adjust until you have achieved a balanced stitch (see Adjusting the Tension for Precise Sewing, page 38).

10. When you are happy with your results, make a note of the settings so you can return to them again and again.

## NEEDLE-UP/DOWN FUNCTION

This handy feature positions the needle and take-up lever in exactly the right position, either needle up or needle down. In the needle up position, the needle is in exactly the right position to start the next seam without tangling. In the needle down position, you can stop the needle down just off the fabric, which allows you to raise and lower the presser foot when piecing without skipping a stitch.

If you don't have a needle-up/down function on your machine, always turn the handwheel toward you to raise or lower the needle. To keep the stitches from tangling when beginning a stitch, make sure the take-up lever is either in the highest or lowest position. To determine this, while turning the handwheel, look at the position of the take up lever, *not* the needle.

## HEADERS AND FOOTERS

Headers and footers are used to begin and end stitching. The header anchors top and bobbin threads, thus preventing them from bunching up under small pieces. These little pieces of fabric are sometimes called *bunny tails* or *leaders* and *enders*.

For headers and footers, I use 4 rectangles (about 1″ × 2″) of light-colored fabric placed wrong sides together. (I like to see the pretty side of the fabric as I sew.) Use any light-colored pieces of fabric—you don't have to use fabric from the quilt you are making.

## Using a Header

**1.** Put 2 rectangles 1″ × 2″ wrong sides together and place them under the presser foot. Holding onto the top and bobbin threads, begin stitching.

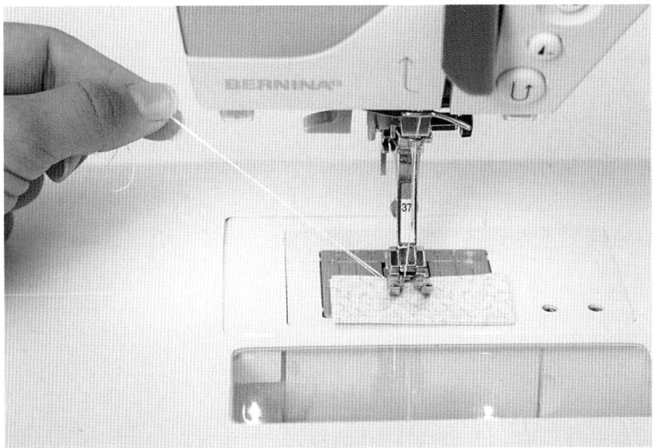

Hold the top and bobbin threads.

**2.** Sew to the end of the fabric. Stop with the needle in the down position just off the edge of the fabric.

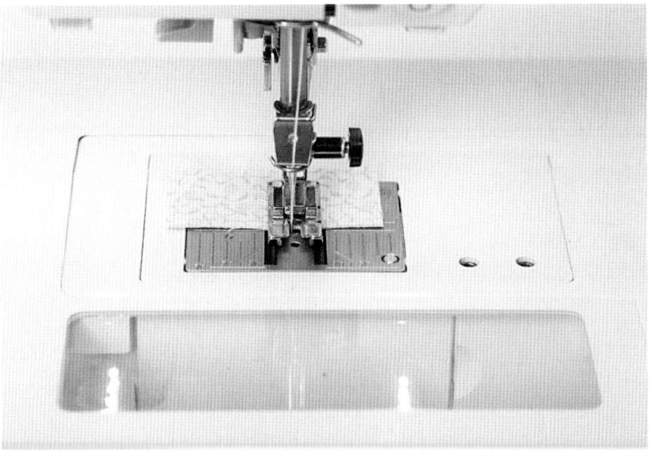

Stop with the needle down and off the edge of the fabric.

**3.** Begin stitching your patchwork.

## Using a Footer

**1.** After chain piecing or other stitching is complete, place a footer under the presser foot and sew to the end, stopping with the needle down just off the edge of the fabric.

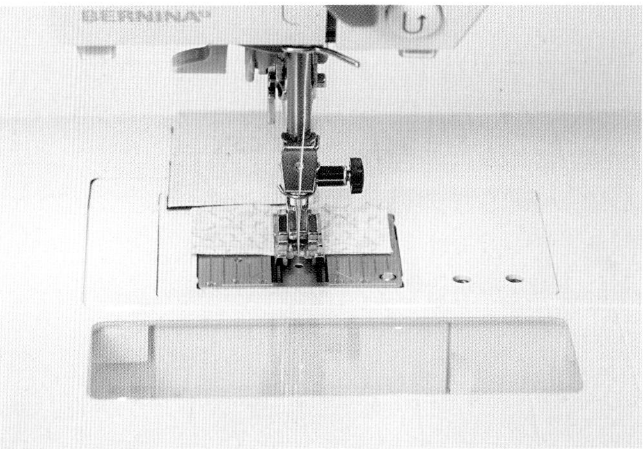

Add a footer after piecing.

**2.** Clip the thread chain that joins the footer to the last piece stitched. Leave the footer under the presser foot with the needle down just off the edge. Now the footer becomes the header.

Clip the thread chain between the footer and the last piece.

**TIP** Making Headers and Footers

When cutting fabric for patchwork, I usually end up with bits of fabric left over. I cut these down to use for headers and footers and keep them in a basket by my sewing machine.

## SEWING ACCURATE SEAMS

Patchwork piecing assumes a ¼″ seam allowance. If the seam allowance is off by as little as ¹⁄₁₆″, then a block that is eight squares wide will be off by ½″. It is important to maintain an accurate, uniform seam allowance from the beginning to the end of all piecing. If the seam is too narrow or too wide, the blocks will not be the correct size and will be difficult to sew together.

**PRECISION PIECING KEY:**

## How to Sew Straight Seams

Sewing consistently straight seams is one of the most challenging precision piecing skills to master. If you have been taught to place both hands on the fabric with one to the left of the presser foot and one to the right of the foot, this is the surest way for the fabric go out of control. The presser foot tends to pull fabric to the left, making it easy to sew in a circle if left unguided. If the left hand is on the fabric, it works as a pivot point; with the right hand on the fabric, it pulls against the left from the opposite side. This positioning of the hands makes it nearly impossible to sew in a straight line, much harder to feed the fabric, and will result in crooked seams. The easiest way to sew straight is to support and feed the fabric, guiding it from the front of the foot and placing a supporting finger along the left side of the presser foot as the last bit of the piece enters under the presser foot.

An awl or similar tool can also be used to help feed the last bit of fabric under the presser foot. I prefer to use my fingers because I can always find them.

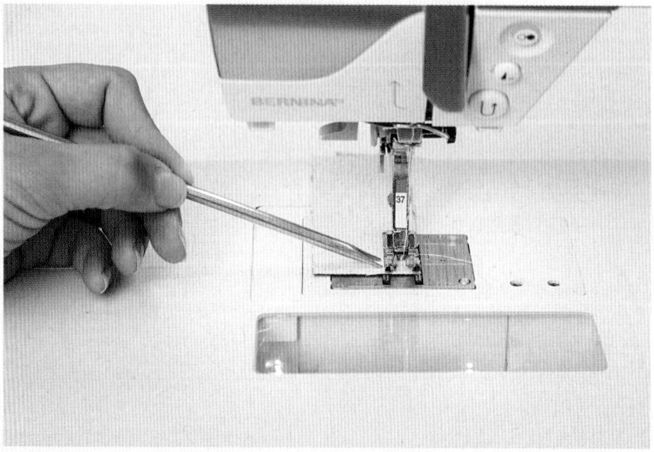


Feeding the last ¼″ of fabric

### Tips for Precision Sewing

- Sit so you can see the edge of the foot rather than the front of the foot. The edge of the foot is where all the action is. You want to make sure that the fabric is being fed consistently along the edge of the foot from beginning to middle to end of the seam. The needle will take care of itself, so no need to be looking there. Just watch the raw edge of the fabric moving along the edge of the foot.
- As you come to the end of the block, it becomes more evident that fabric tends to be pushed to the left, thus resulting in a narrower seam allowance at the bottom. To avoid this, put your middle finger or awl on the fabric right along the left edge of the foot. If using your finger, apply pressure against the foot and on the fabric, so the fabric cannot escape from the edge of the foot. Slow down at the end, making sure the fabric remains along the edge of the foot.

## PATCHWORK FOOT GUIDE VERSUS NO GUIDE

I prefer to stitch without a guide on my patchwork foot. I can see exactly where the raw edge of the fabric is along the edge the foot and make minor adjustments as I sew, especially at the beginning and end of a seam.

I have taught a lot of classes on precision piecing. During the class, students cut and sew to find their precise patchwork seam. By the end of the lesson, most of the students with a guide on their patchwork foot ended up removing the guide, having found that it blocked the view of the fabric along the edge of the foot and got in the way of their precision. Once they removed the guide and resewed the seams, their blocks came out the correct size.

Some sewing machines come with an even-feed system that is always (or can be) engaged when desired. If your machine has an even-feed system, I highly recommend using it when piecing. I do not recommend using a walking foot for piecing, only for quilting.

## PRECISION PIECING: A NO-PINNING APPROACH

If you want to sew along:

1. Select a light fabric and a dark fabric.

2. Cut 2 strips 1½″ × 4½″ from the dark fabric.

3. Cut 1 strip 1½″ × 4½″ from the light fabric.

Accurate seam preparation is a key to precision piecing—using glue instead of pins allows for more precision because pins, even fine ones, can distort your fabric. For this technique, you need basting glue (page 16) and color-coded clips (page 16).

### Basting Fabrics Together with Basting Glue

Make sure the pieces are lined up exactly by checking the front and the back of the strips before pressing. I am often surprised to see that two pieces that appear well aligned from the front are actually not lined up when I check the back. Take the time to adjust when necessary. If the fabric is not lined up exactly all along the edge, the seam allowance will be inconsistent.

1. Position a dark strip right side up on your ironing surface.

2. Put little dots of basting glue along the long edge of the dark strip in the seam allowance.

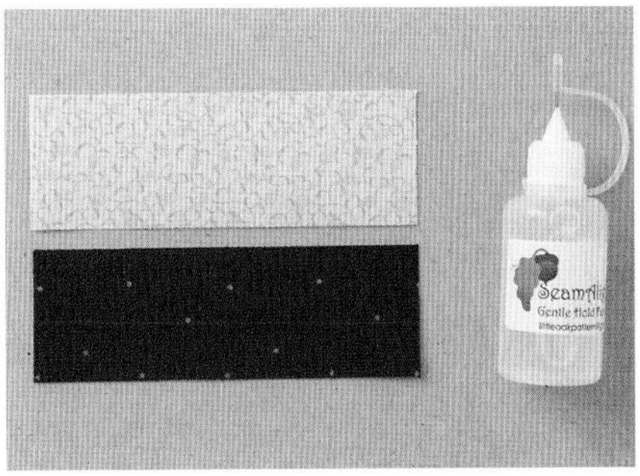

Place little dots of glue in the seam allowance.

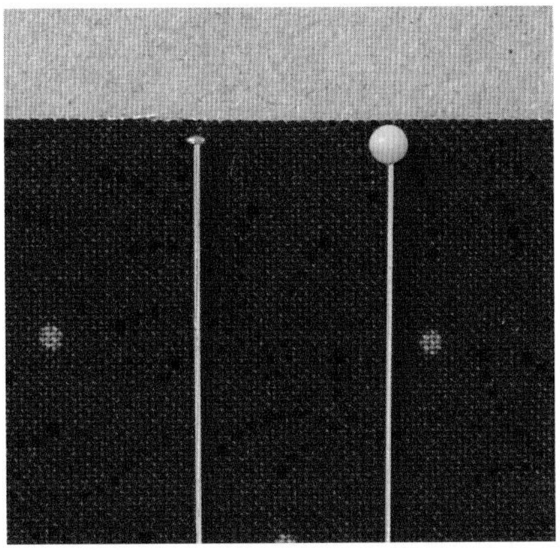

Dots the size of steel pinhead just right. Dots the size of glass pinhead too big.

3. Place the light strip on top of the dark strip right sides together, lining up seams exactly.

4. Press for about 10 seconds to set the glue.

5. Fasten a color-coded clip on the glued edge to serve as a reminder of the edge you glued.

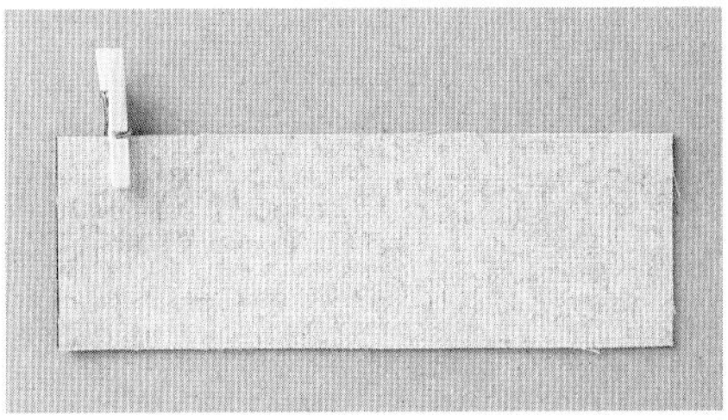

Seams aligned exactly with the color coded clip on the glued edge

Don't worry, if you want to press the seams open or must remove a seam, the glue releases effortlessly.

## Sewing the Seams

**1.** Sew onto a header (see Headers and Footers, page 40), stopping with the needle down at the end.

**2.** Remove the color-coded clip, slightly raise the presser foot, and snug the strip up to the needle, lining up the raw edges with the edge of the presser foot.

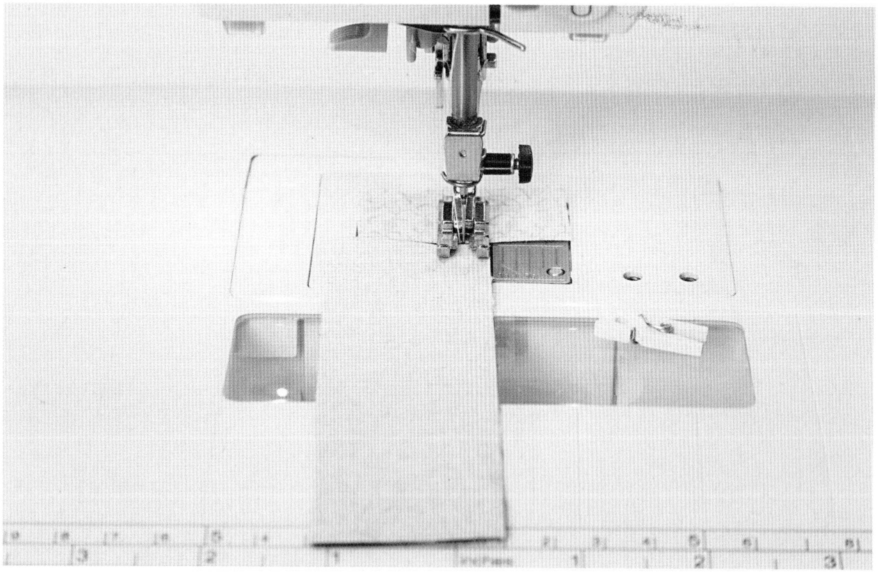

Remove color-coded clips before starting to sew.

**3.** Begin stitching slowly along the edge of the fabric, allowing the feed dogs to feed the fabric. Keep the strip feeding straight along the edge of the foot from beginning to end.

**TIP** Remove the color-coded clip before stitching and place back on the strip after stitching. This is a good habit to get into.

**4.** When you reach the end of the strip, stitch onto a footer, stop with the needle down, and snip the thread chain between the strip and the footer.

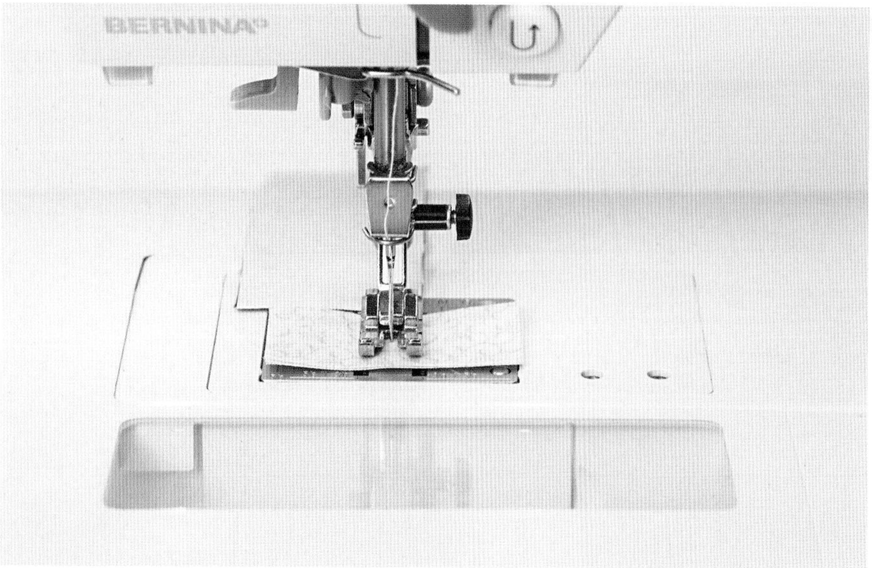


Sewing onto the footer

**NOTE: Important**

*Before sewing on the second dark strip, follow the setting, pressing, stabilizing, and flattening steps below for the first two strips.*

## Setting and Pressing Seams

**1.** After stitching, place the unit on the pressing surface just as it came out of the sewing machine. Place the iron on top of the seam for about 5 seconds.

**2.** Place the strip with the fabric you are pressing the seams toward on top, seams parallel and facing toward you.

**3.** Lift the top fabric up and over the stitches.

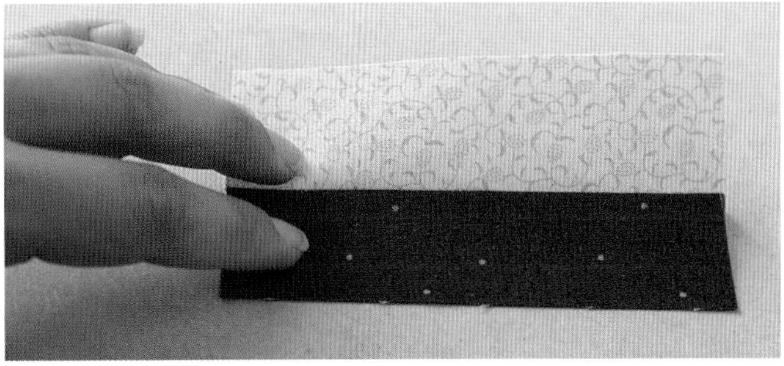

Lift fabric over stitches.

**4.** Begin in the center of the strip and finger press the fabric up to and along the stitches, working from the center to the left, then from the center to the right.

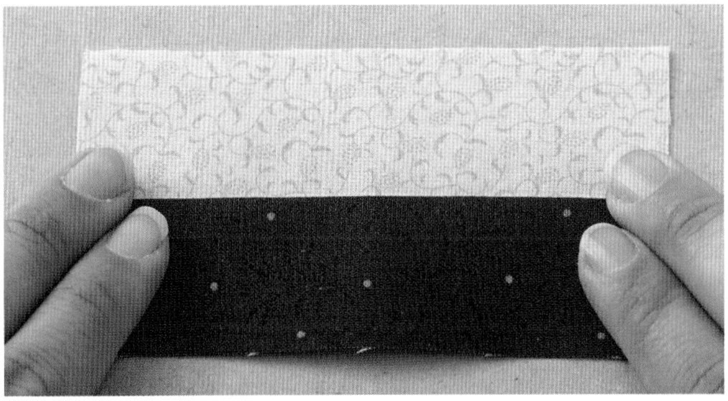

Finger pressing

**5.** Keeping gentle pressure on the fabric at the stitches with the fingers of your left hand, place the iron on the strips equally distributed on both strips.

**6.** Press from right to left, gently sliding the iron and your fingers horizontally along the seam. Apply only enough pressure with your fingers and iron to mold the fabric to the stitches without stretching the strip out of shape.

Press gently.

## STABILIZING AND FLATTENING SEAMS WITH STARCH ALTERNATIVE

For this process, use an applicator pen or paintbrush and starch alternative (page 17). I prefer the Easy Press Pen and Easy Press Solution (page 17). If you do not have an applicator pen, you can pour a small amount of starch alternative into a small container and use a paintbrush to apply it.

**1.** Apply the starch alternative to the high side of the seam, using your applicator pen or paintbrush. You should see a light film of starch alternative on the fabric. Place the iron on top of the seam and press to dry.

**2.** Press and starch each seam as you go.

- Pressing to dry takes about 5–7 seconds depending on the heat of your iron.
- Starch alternative is applied directly to the seam exactly where you want it to be. This makes subcutting strips, units, and trimming HSTs much easier and far more accurate, as the seam is flat and there is less stretching.
- If there is a shine on the fabric from pressing, it will wash out when you wash the finished quilt.

Apply a light film of starch alternative to the high side of the seam.

## USING A STARCH ALTERNATIVE APPLICATOR

**1.** Fill the applicator pen with starch alternative, being careful not to overfill. Prime by pressing about ten times on the nib. Once primed, the nib will remain sufficiently damp for applying a light film of starch to a few seams, depending on the length of the seams. The more practice you have with the pen, the more it will become evident when it is time to prime again. When time to prime again two presses on the nib will be sufficient.

**2.** Use the applicator pen as though it is a highlighter, holding it at a 45° angle with the wide edge of the nib on the high side of the fabric. Apply gentle pressure, so as to not stretch the fabric, and draw the nib along the high side of the fabric from left to right (reverse if left-handed).

If the fabric is shifting under the nib, too much pressure being applied. Decrease the pressure until the fabric is not shifting.

**NOTE: Important**

*For the final seam, add the next strip, using the same process as sewing the first seam.*

## MEASURING FOR ACCURACY

- If the strip set is wider than 3½″ and the center strip is wider than 1″, your seam allowance needs to be wider.
- If the strip set is narrower than 3½″ and the center strip is narrower than 1″, your seam allowance needs to be narrower.
- Make the necessary adjustments to your seam allowance and repeat the process until you have an accurate strip set (see Sewing Accurate Seams, page 42).

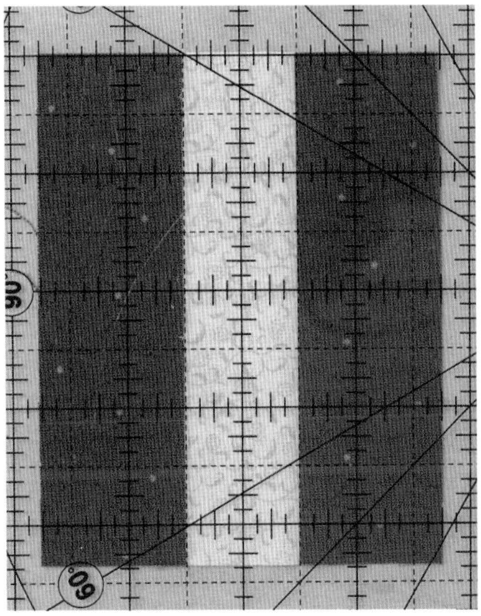

Precise seams

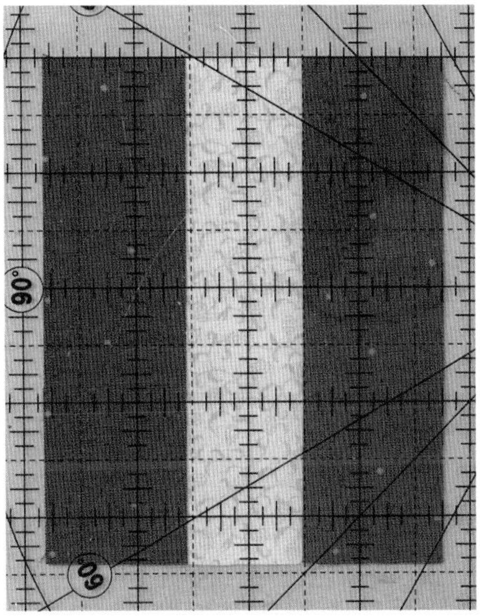

Seams too narrow

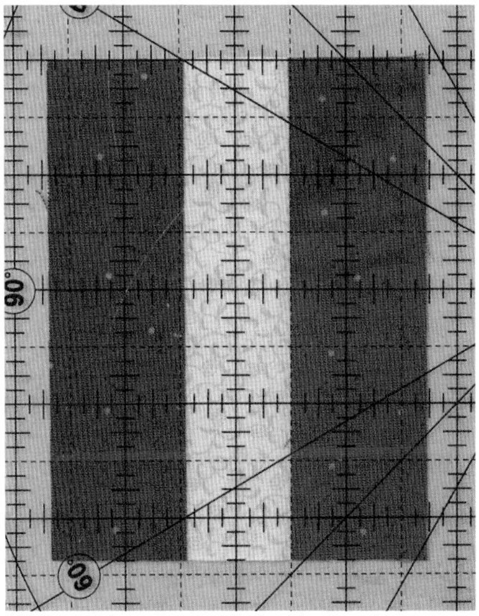

Seams too wide

When you have achieved a precise patchwork seam, including even tension and stitch length (see Stitch Length for Precision Piecing, page 40) with the right thread and needle (see Notions and Supplies, page 15), make a note of these important details.

**TIP** When piecing with batiks or flannels, you may find that your seam allowance is too wide or narrow and you will need to adjust accordingly. I highly recommend following the above steps to find your precise patchwork seam when working with different weights of fabric.

## PRECISION VERSUS PERFECTION

Precision and perfection do not mean the same thing. The two words are related in that they describe a high degree of excellence, but both are independent of one another. *Perfection* suggests something that is flawless. *Precision* is about accuracy and the ability to reproduce a measurement consistently.

Quilting is a creative process and encompasses all personalities. For some it is not important to have every seam and point match, while for others it is crucial. It is worthwhile to know where you fall within that spectrum and to set the standard for yourself.

Aiming for precision takes practice, making a concise and consistent effort to be accurate in every detail. If you have set a high standard for yourself, focus on getting as good as you can possibly be while striving for progress toward accuracy.

I have found that the pursuit of perfection in my own work sabotages the flow of creativity. Rather than seeking perfection, I set my sights on achieving a standard of excellence in piecing that meets my own standards, and I find joy in working toward achieving them. If a seam does not match precisely, I evaluate the results, asking myself whether or not it will bother me if I leave it as it is. If my answer is yes, it will bother me, I remove the seam and try again. If my answer is no, it will not bother me, I will leave it as it is. If uncertain, I set the block aside for later evaluation.

## NOTES ON FINGER PRESSING AND PRESSING WITH AN IRON

When I first started quilting, I took a class on how to make a Snowball quilt. In this class I learned how to sew bias corners onto a square and press. After making my Snowball blocks, I wanted to impress my teacher with well-pressed corners, so I started steaming, pulling, and pressing. The more I steamed, pulled, and pressed, the more the bias stretched and distorted; yet I anxiously kept at it, trying to flatten those mangled corners. Suddenly from a far back corner of the room, I heard my teacher's frantic voice calling out, "Shelley! Step away from the fabric!" That was the day I learned the important lesson of proper pressing.

As with each step from preparing fabric (page 24) to cutting and piecing, proper pressing is vital to the overall results of your patchwork. I have seen pieced units that are precisely cut and pieced only to end up damaged by the pressing process.

- Press seams to one side: When left exposed, seams are vulnerable to many outside forces that can cause them to weaken and break. With seams pressed to the side, the thread is protected by the fabric.
- After pressing seams to one side, a narrow ridge of fabric will remain along the path of the thread. This ridge plays an important role in precision piecing: Two units of pieced patchwork nested together at the seams will form a precise match.
- Setting seams and finger pressing are essential. Setting the seam settles the thread, nestles the stitches into the fabric, smooths out any waves caused during stitching, and makes the unit lie flatter. Finger pressing helps mold the fabric to the stitches before pressing with the iron.
- When finger pressing, avoid scraping your fingernails horizontally along the seam, as this may create little pleats along the seam, and the extra pressure exerted can stretch and distort your strips. Use only your fingertips to press up to and against a seam.
- Strips should remain straight on your pressing surface with no gap between fabric and thread, no creases, and no stitches showing at the seam.
- If a strip is warped or stretched out of shape with stitches showing at the seam, too much pressure is being applied along the seam. Ease off on the pressure until you have a strip that is straight, with the fabric rolled over on top of the stitches and with no stitches showing. This takes a bit of practice, but once you have the feel of the amount of pressure to apply with your fingertips and iron, you will be able to repeat the same pressure over and over again with the results of a nice straight strip of patchwork in front of you.

**PRECISION PIECING KEY:**

# Quick Reference Guide for Precision Piecing

- To keep the thread from creating a thread nest, begin stitching on a header (see Headers and Footers, page 40).
- Position the fabric under the presser foot snug up to the needle, lining up the raw edges with the edge of the presser foot.
- Begin stitching slowly at the top edge of the fabric. No need to backstitch. Guiding fabric from the front, let the machine do all the feeding. Avoid pushing or pulling the fabric. Stitch along the edge of the piece slowly so you have control in guiding the fabric. Keep your eyes on the right edge of the fabric, guiding the fabric from the front of the foot and keeping the raw edge of the fabric along the right edge of the presser foot (see Precision Piecing Key: How to Sew Straight Seams, page 42).
- When you reach the end of the seam, stop with the needle down just off the edge of the fabric, lift the presser foot about ⅛″, add a footer (see Headers and Footers, page 40), stop with the needle down off the edge of the footer, and snip the thread between the footer and the strip pieces.
- Fabric tends to be pushed to the left when nearing the end of a seam. To keep the last bit of fabric feeding straight under the presser foot, place your index or middle finger on the fabric and apply pressure against the left edge of the presser foot, while still allowing the feed dogs to evenly feed the fabric.
- If the fabric is creating a "bow wave" in front of the foot stop, put the needle down, slightly raise the presser foot about ⅛″, adjust the fabric, lower the presser foot, and continue sewing.
- Always set the seam as it came out of the machine. Press as you go and before adding another piece.
- If pressing several strips or units at a time, set up an assembly line. Lay out the units that can fit on your pressing area and set the seams. Allow them to cool, and then begin pressing the seams to one side. Repeat until you have pressed all the strips or units.
- When possible, sew with the unpieced unit on top and the pieced unit on the bottom.

Creating quality work takes time and focus. At first, learning these new techniques may seem to take a lot of time, but soon it will become the norm and you will speed up.

Adding these new techniques to your repertoire will improve accuracy, provide you with consistently good results and fewer mistakes, and bring precision to every step of piecing.

## CHAIN PIECING

For efficiency, nothing beats chain piecing.

**1.** Start with a header (see Headers and Footers, page 40), sew to the end, and stop with the needle down just off the edge of the fabric.

**2.** Slightly raise the presser foot, about ⅛″ is plenty, place the next piece up to the needle, lining up raw edges with the edge of the presser foot, lower the presser foot, and start sewing.

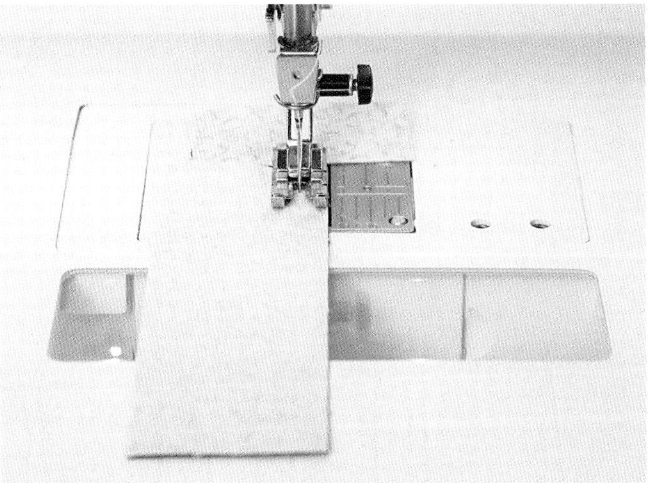

Sew from a header onto the strips.

**3.** Sew to the end of the piece, raise the presser foot, and add the next piece.

Sew from one set of strips to the next.

**4.** After all the pieces have been sewn, add a footer, stop with the needle down, off the edge of the footer, and snip the thread between the pieces and the footer.

**TIP** Chain Piecing Tips

- When raising the presser foot to place the next piece, you need only enough space to slide the patchwork up to the needle.
- One stitch between the pieces is plenty. If you stitch beyond the edge of the fabric the feed dogs will come into contact with your presser foot and cause damage over time. The contact with the feed dogs will create grooves on the underside of the presser foot. These grooves will create feeding problems, such as varying stitch lengths and wandering fabric, which will affect accuracy.
- If your machine came provided with a Free-Hand System (FHS) / knee lift, now is the time to get used to it. The FHS / knee lift allows you to raise and lower the presser foot without using your hands while piecing, saving time and improving accuracy.
- Some of the new computerized machines have a hover setting that slightly raises the presser foot when you stop stitching, leaving your hands free while sewing. The hover feature works only when the needle is set to stop in the down position.

## BLOCK ASSEMBLY PRESSING STATION

When assembling blocks, the same small area on your ironing board gets pressed repeatedly. Protect your pressing surface from stains and discoloration that can occur from repetitive pressing, starching, and gluing with an appliqué pressing sheet (page 13) and pressing cloth. Another benefit is that the pressing sheet generates more heat so the glue and starch dry faster.

**1.** Center an appliqué pressing sheet on your ironing surface.

**2.** Cover with a plain, light-colored 100% cotton fabric.

**3.** Tape fabric to the pressing surface with double-sided tape.

**TIP** Keep Your Pressing Cloth Clean

Change the pressing cloth when it gets overly stained or discolored. I have several pressing cloths; when one is ready to be changed, I replace it with another and wash so it is ready the next time I need it. Basting glue and starch alternative are easily removed from the surface of the pressing cloth in the wash. When stains have set in from the heat of the iron and the cloth no longer comes out clean, I toss it and replace it with a new one.

# CORRECTING MISTAKES

## Easing Fabric Between Seams

Sometimes no matter how accurately you cut, press, and sew, you may need to ease fabric between seams.

**1.** After lining up the seams and matching corners, if one fabric is bigger than the other, place a drop of basting glue in the center of the smaller piece.

**2.** Line up the center of the larger piece to the center of the smaller piece and press to dry. If more easing is needed, add drops of basing glue between the layers of fabric and press to dry, until both pieces are nicely lined up.

**3.** Remove color-coded clips, place the block on the ironing surface, and press to dry.

**4.** Stitch with the piece that needs to be eased in on the bottom. This way the feed dogs will help ease in the excess fabric.

## Removing Seams

Fabric stretches and gives. Tiny little inconsistencies will always exist in patchwork and in my opinion add charm to your work. Go easy on yourself, learn from your mistakes, and choose what is important to remove and what can stay. Slow down and enjoy the journey, the process of learning new techniques, and doing your best work. Above all, celebrate your creativity.

To remove stitches:

**1.** Cut every third or fourth stitch.

**2.** Turn the piece over and remove the long thread from behind.

**3.** Use tweezers to pull out the little pieces of threads that remain.

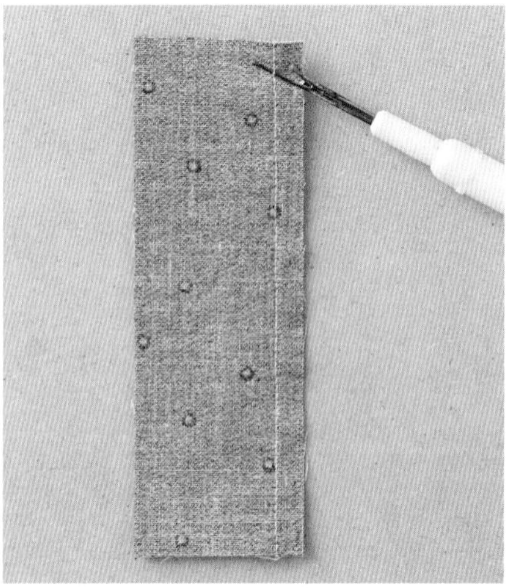

Cut thread at intervals.

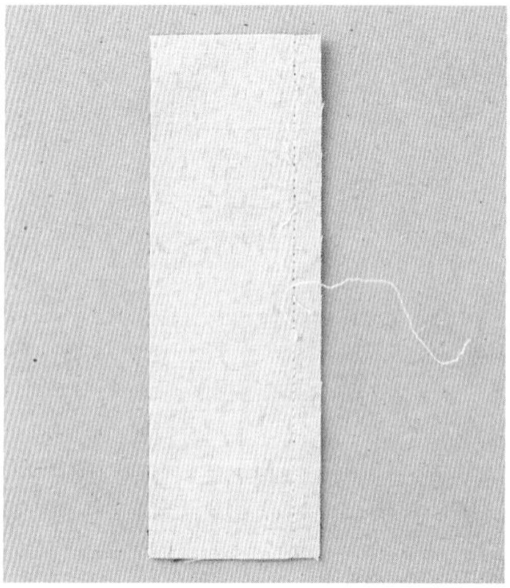

Remove the thread.

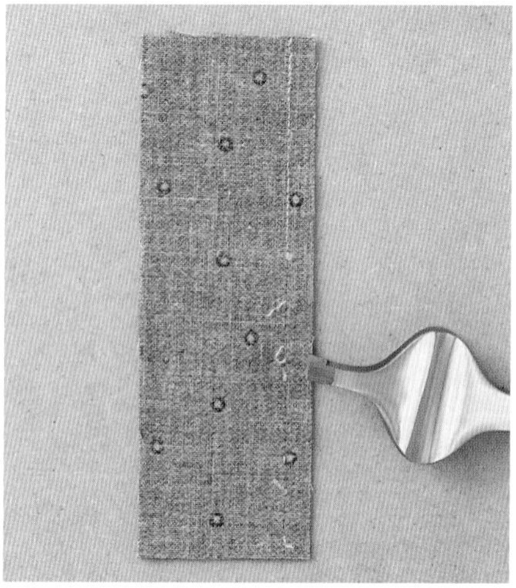

Remove the little pieces of thread.

After removing stitches, you will notice that there are little holes left behind from the needle. Paint a thin layer of starch alternative over top of the holes and press to dry. The starch plumps up the fibers and fills the holes.

Handle your fabric gently when removing seams. This way, if you find the need to remove seams more than once, the fabrics will not fray or stretch out of shape.

## Changing the Direction of a Pressed Seam

If you need to change the direction of a seam you pressed, simply press the seam flat again as though it just came out of the machine, apply a thin layer of starch alternative along the seam on the wrong side of the fabric, press to dry, and then press the seam in the correct direction.

# MAKING PRECISION-PIECED BLOCKS

*For basic techniques, see The Precise Patchwork Seam (page 38). All measurements include ¼″ seams.*

Now that you know how to sew a precise patchwork seam, it's time to move ahead to making precise blocks. If you want to practice making these blocks, make a copy of the appropriate Quilt Block Builder to work with; otherwise, just read along and refer back to these pages when making your projects.

**PRECISION PIECING KEY:**

## Precision Piecing Guidelines

- Whenever possible, cut fabric for the units one thread larger than indicated in the pattern, sew them together, and then trim them down to size. Working with larger pieces and trimming them down makes more accurate finished units, which leads to more accurate finished blocks.
- After the units are sewn together into a block, never trim down the finished block. Trimming a finished block removes seam allowances that are needed to keep points sharp and squares square. Instead, measure the units within the block to see if anything went wrong. If you find inaccuracies you cannot live with, take the block apart, fix the area where the problem occurred, and sew the block back together.
- Measure each unit as you go, and make certain it is the right size before sewing it into a block. This way you can spot and fix any problems before the block is sewn together. This is a good habit to get into, laying a good foundation for when you start making more complicated blocks.

## FOUR-PATCH BLOCK

Make a copy of the Practice Four-Patch Quilt Block Builder (pullout page P2) and prepare a Quilt Block Base (page 8). Color in the positioning circles to match your colored clips.

A Four-Patch block is created by combining 2 two-patch units.

### Cutting Strips

*See Precision Cutting (page 31).*

Use the same background print and two different main prints for the strip sets.

**1.** Cut 2 light 1½″ × 2″ strips.

**2.** Cut 2 dark 1½″ × 2″ strips.

### Sewing Strips

*See The Precise Patchwork Seam (page 38).*

**1.** Sew a dark strip to a light strip. Make 2.

**2.** Press the seams toward the dark fabric.

**3.** Measure the strip sets. They should measure 2½″ × 2″.

## Subcutting Strip Sets

Use two rulers that are 6″ × 12″.

**1.** Place a strip set right side up on your cutting mat with the seam horizontal.

**2.** Line up one ruler along the horizontal seam and butt the other ruler up to it, covering the uneven edge approximately ⅛″.

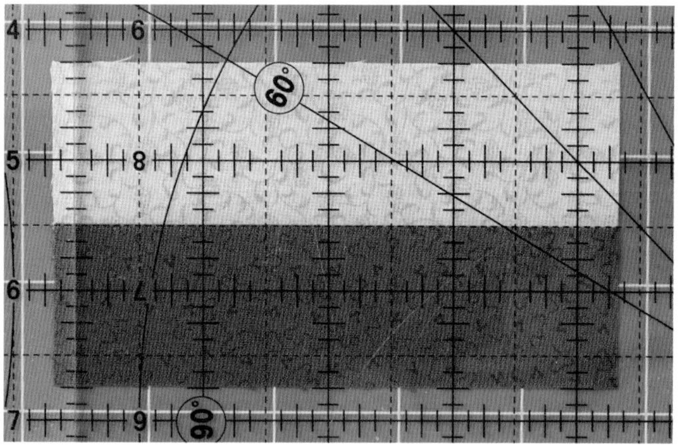

Line up rulers for subcutting.

**3.** Move aside the first ruler and make the first cut to remove the uneven edges.

Move aside first ruler.

**4.** Slide the ruler over so the 1½″ line is lined up on top of the cut edge and a horizontal line is lined up along the seam, and then cut a 1½″ strip set. Repeat Steps 1–3 for the remaining strip set.

After trimming left edge, move ruler over to cut two-patch units.

**5.** Attach a color-coded clip of the same color as its color-coded position on the Quilt Block Builder.

**6.** Arrange the units onto the Quilt Block Builder.

Color-coded clip matches color-coded positioning circle on Quilt Block Builder.

## Nesting Seams

*Nesting seams* refers to butting two opposing seams together when lining them up for piecing. Opposing the seams makes it easy to match and nest two seams together. Press the seams on your strips toward the dark fabric, and when the two units are placed right sides together, the seams will naturally oppose. To ensure the pieces will be matched at the seam, line up and nest the seams below the ¼″ seam allowance, *not* just at the very top.

**TIP** Nesting Seams

When new to patchwork, it can be difficult to know what two seams feel like when they are nested together. Practice holding a pair of 2 patches together nested at the seam.

1. Feel along the length of the seam, and make a mental note of how the seam feels.

2. Move the seams apart, creating a narrow gap between them. Feel along the seam—you should be able to feel the gap between the seams.

3. Place the seams on top of one another and feel along the seam—you should feel more bulk along the seam.

4. Nest the seams together again and feel along the seam. Now you should be able to feel the seams accurately lined up with one another.

## Sewing the Block Together

1. Center the units right sides together with dark to light and light to dark; match and nest the seams.

Nested seams

2. Insert the narrow tip of basting glue applicator between the two pieces and apply a small dot of glue in the seam allowance along the low side of the seam.

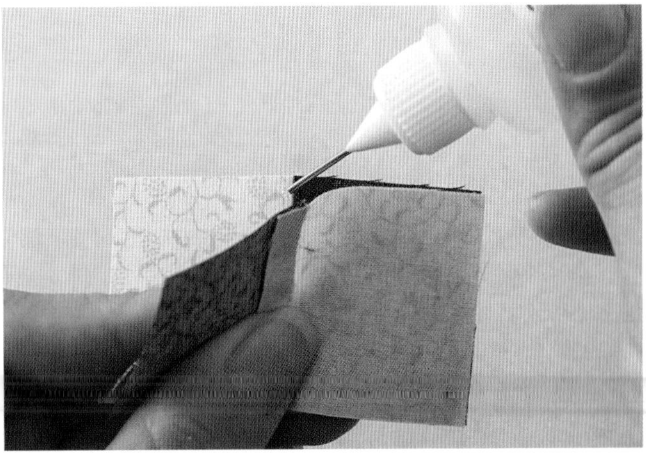

Apply basting glue.

**3.** Fasten a color-coded clip over the seams.

Fasten clip.

**4.** Place a drop of basting glue on one corner and line up the corners.

Apply basting glue to corner.

**5.** Repeat Step 4 for the remaining corner.

**6.** Remove the color-coded clip and press to dry.

**7.** Begin stitching, and when you reach the nested seams, slow down and place a finger or awl on the seam allowance to keep it from moving to the left. Make sure to keep the same seam allowance from beginning to middle to end.

## Fanning Seams

*Fanning seams*, also known as *spinning seams*, helps to reduce the bulk of several seams converging together.

**1.** Hold the block in your left and right hand with the long seam horizontal. This horizontal seam is the last seam you stitched.

**2.** Use your left thumb to push the seam down on the left side and your right thumb to push the seam up on the right side.

**3.** You will notice the stitches in the seam allowance release, which allows the seams to be pressed in opposite directions.

You will know you have fanned the seams correctly when you see a tiny four-patch appear in the center where the seams intersect.

Fan seams.

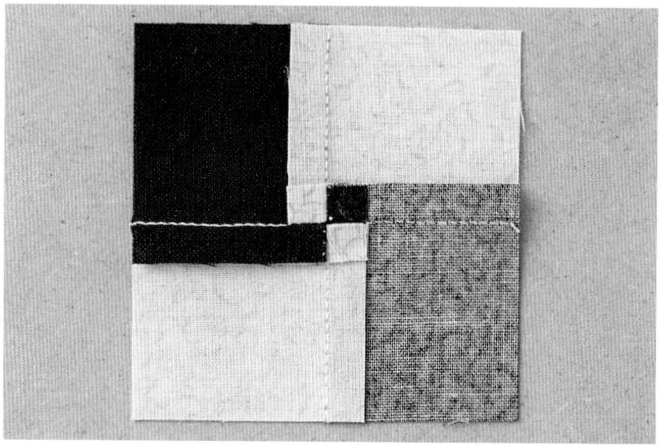

Correctly fanned seams appear as a tiny four-patch.

**4.** Place the block wrong side up on your pressing surface and finger press the tiny four-patch so it lies flat.

**5.** Turn the block right side up, finger press the seams, and press with an iron.

**6.** Apply a thin film of starch alternative along the seams and press to dry.

**TIP** **Pressing**

For best results, always press each seam as you go.

## Trimming the Block

**1.** Place the Four-Patch block on your mat right side up.

**2.** Using a 6″ × 6″ square or 6″ × 12″ rectangle ruler, line up the vertical 1¼″ line on the ruler along the vertical seam and a horizontal line along the horizontal seam.

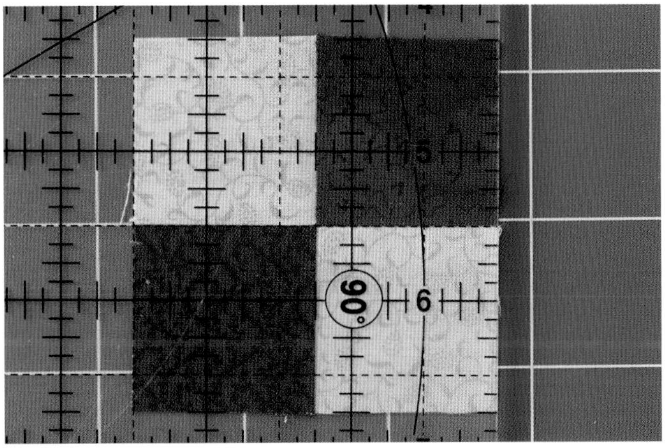


Position ruler for trimming.

**3.** Trim any fabric that extends beyond the right edge of the ruler.

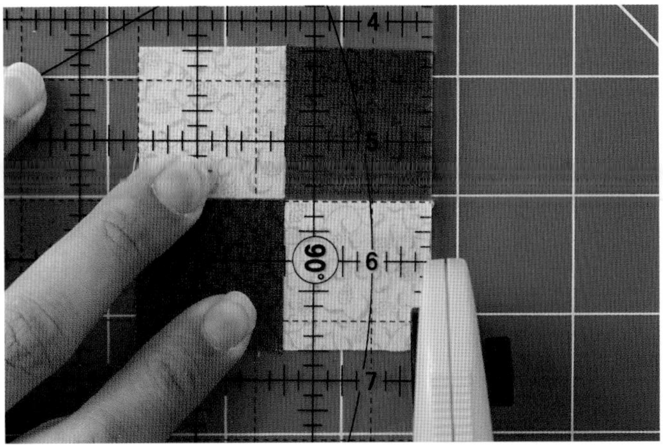


Trim.

**4.** Working in a clockwise manner, repeat Steps 2 and 3 until all 4 edges have been trimmed.

**5.** Place the Four-Patch block under the ruler and check to see that it measures exactly 2½″ × 2½″.

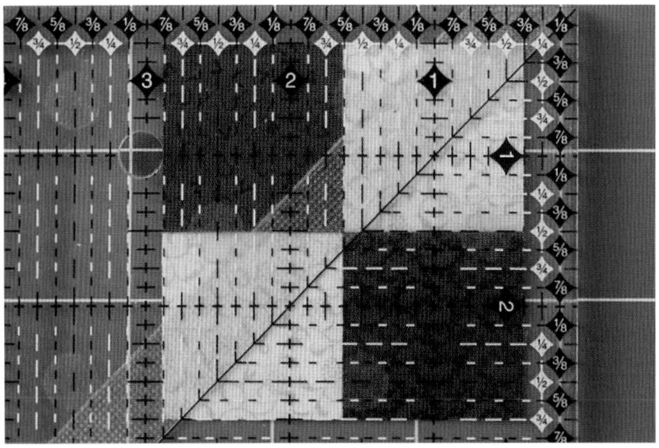

Block should measure exactly 2½″ × 2½″.

If your block is does not measure 2½″ × 2½″, now is the time to evaluate where things went wrong. Check your seam allowance and trimming. Fix the mistake and try again.

Finished block on its Quilt Block Builder

**TIP** Trimming

When trimming, if the fabric is pushed away from the cutter at the top right corner, it can result in an inaccurate cut. To avoid this, start cutting the fabric at the top corner, rolling the blade toward you, and cut about ½″ down. Then, start the cut at the bottom, rolling the blade away from you to finish the cut.

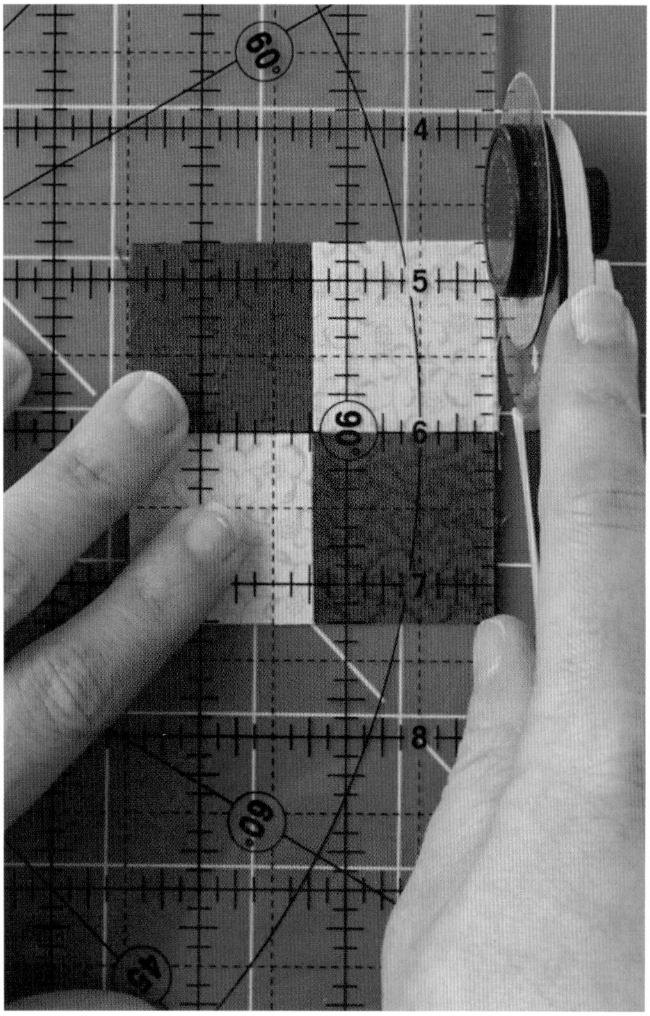

Begin cutting at the top right corner, rolling the blade toward you.

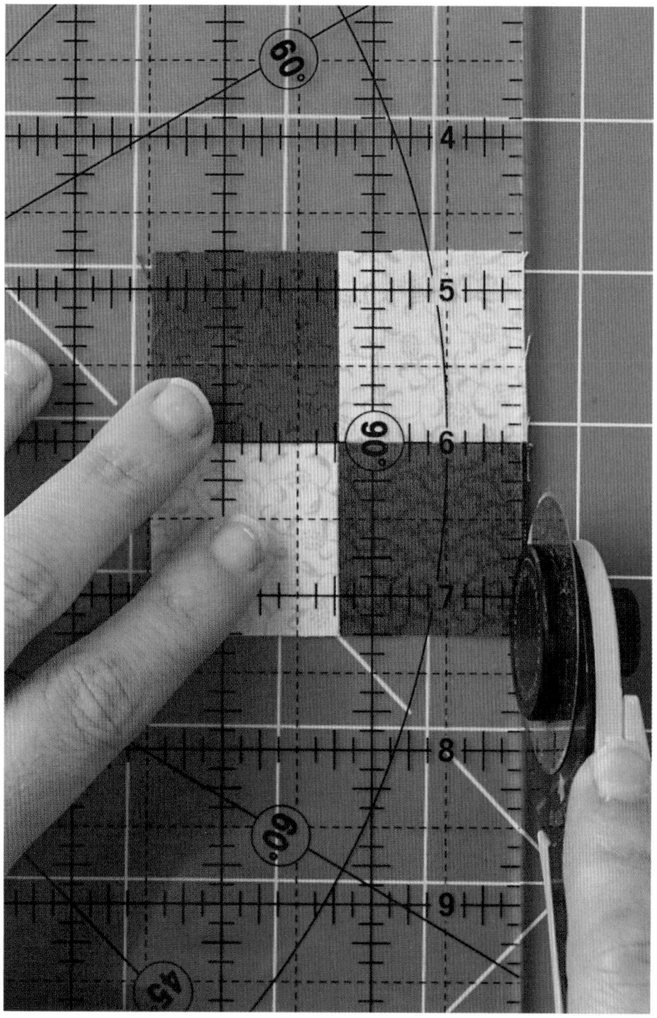

End cutting from the bottom right corner, rolling the blade away from you.

## NINE-PATCH BLOCK

Make a copy of the Practice Nine-Patch Quilt Block Builder (pullout page P2) and prepare a Quilt Block Base (page 8). Color in the positioning circles to match your colored clips.

A Nine-Patch block is created by combining 3 three-patch units.

### Cutting Strips

*See Precision Cutting (page 31).*

**1.** Cut 5 dark strips 1½″ × 4″.

**2.** Cut 4 light strips 1½″ × 4″.

**3.** Arrange the strips in order on the Quilt Block Builder.

Arrange the strips.

### Making Strip Sets

*See The Precise Patchwork Seam (page 38).*

**1.** Make 2 dark-light-dark strip sets.

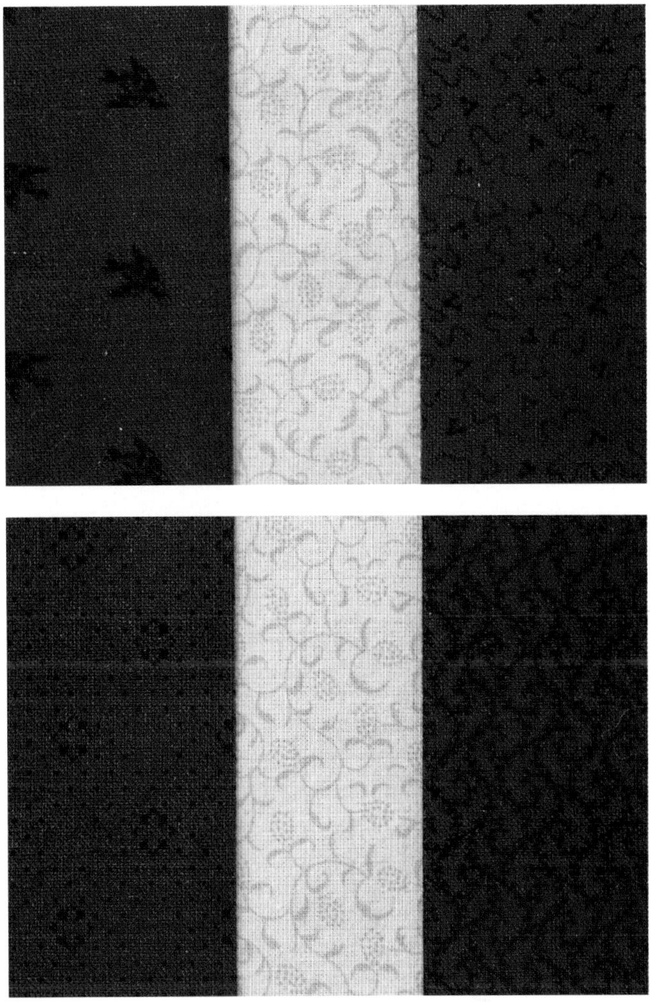

Make dark-light-dark strip sets.

**2.** Make 1 light-dark-light strip set.

Make light-dark-light strip set.

3. Place dark and light strips right sides together, glue, and press with the iron.

4. Attach a matching color-coded clip to the glued edge of each strip.

Match color-coded clip to the Quilt Block Builder positioning circles.

5. Chain piece (page 51) the three strip sets.

**TIP** After sewing a strip set be sure to reattach the color-coded clip to the edge.

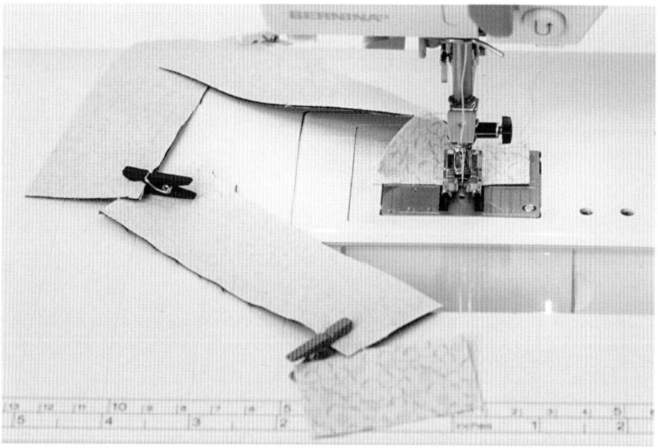
Reattach color-coded clip to edge after sewing.

6. Remove a color-coded clip, press the seams toward the dark fabric, and reattach the clip to the top of the strip.

7. Arrange the strips on the Quilt Block Builder placing matching color-coded clips with positioning circle.

8. Add the remaining strip to each of the 3 strip sets and attach the matching color-coded clip to the glued edge.

Matching color-coded clip attached to the glued edge of the strips.

9. Chain piece the 3 strip sets. Press the seams toward the dark fabric. Reattach the color-coded clip to the strips.

## Subcutting Strip Sets

*Use the two-ruler method for cutting (see Squaring Up Yardage, page 34).*

**1.** Place the top row strip set right side up on your cutting mat with the seams horizontal.

**2.** Remove the color-coded clip and set it aside while cutting.

**3.** Line up one ruler along the horizontal seams and butt the other up to it covering the uneven edge plus ⅛″.

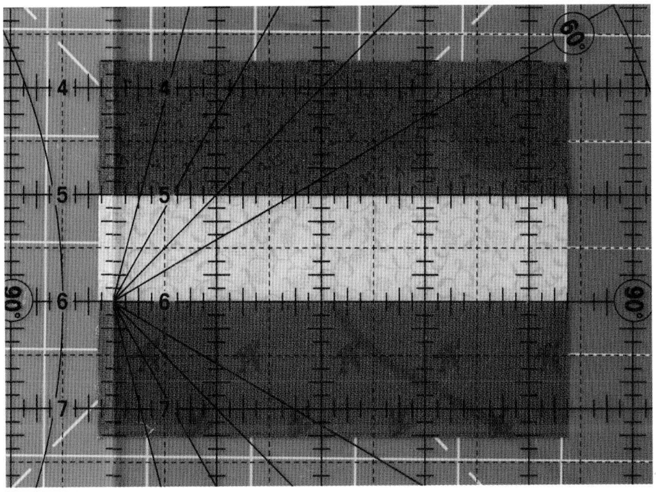

Line up ruler.

**4.** Move aside the first ruler and make the first cut to remove the uneven edges.

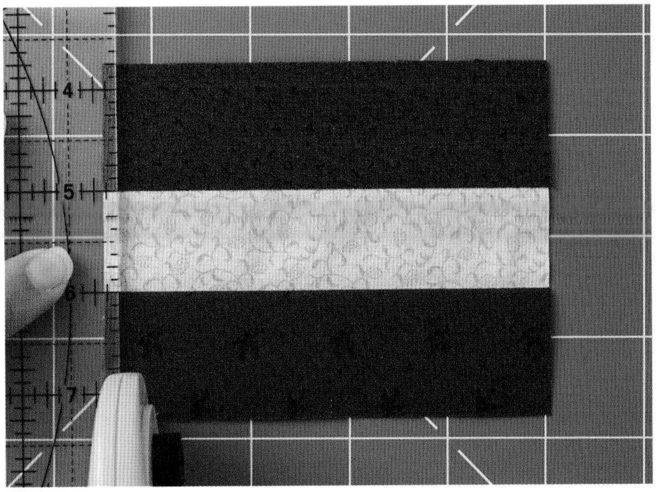

Move first ruler aside.

**5.** Slide the ruler over so the 1½″ line is lined up on top of the cut edge and the horizontal lines are lined up along the seams.

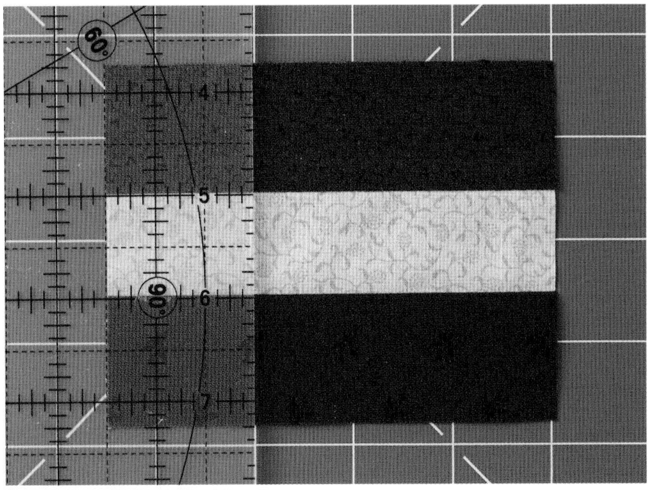

Slide ruler over.

**6.** Cut a 1½″ strip. Attach a color-coded clip to the top center of the strip and place in the top row of the Quilt Block Builder.

Cut the strip.

**7.** Repeat Steps 1–6 for the remaining 2 strip sets.

## Sewing the Block Together

**1.** Center the top and center strip sets right sides together with dark to light and light to dark, matching raw edges and nesting seams (page 55).

**2.** Where the first 2 seams are nested, insert the narrow tip of basting glue applicator between the 2 strip sets. Apply a small dot of glue in the seam allowance along the low side of the seam. Fasten a color-coded clip over the seams.

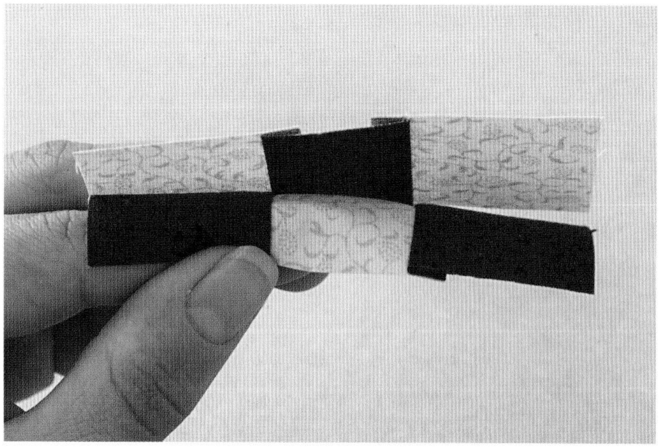

Apply basting glue.

**3.** Move to the next seam, apply a drop of basting glue along the low side of the seam, and fasten a color-coded clip over the seams.

Apply basting glue and clips.

**4.** Place a drop of basting glue on one corner, line up the corners, and press to dry. Repeat for the remaining corner.

**5.** Remove the color-coded clip and press.

**6.** Begin stitching. Slow down as you approach the nested seams. Keep the edge of the fabric lined up with the edge of the presser foot from the beginning, over the seams and to the end.

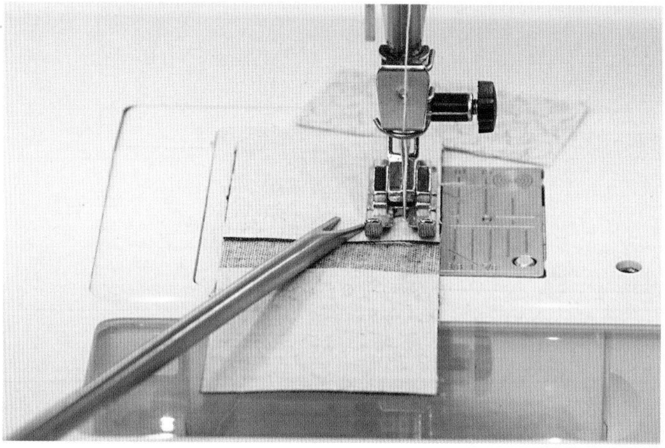

Carefully stitch the seam.

**7.** Set the seam, finger press the seams toward the center strips, and press with the iron.

**8.** Apply a thin film of starch alternative and press to dry.

Apply starch alternative.

**9.** Sew the bottom strip set to the center strip set, repeating Steps 1–8.

Nine-Patch block on its Quilt Block Builder

**10.** If your block does not measure 3½″ × 3½″, find where the problem occurred and fix it.

## HALF-SQUARE TRIANGLES (HSTs) AND PINWHEELS

The following technique uses two squares to make two half-square triangle units. This technique is easy and very accurate, and best of all, the bias remains inside of the square and the straight grain outside (see Watch Out for Bias Edges, page 31).

Use the chart below to make HSTs in a variety of sizes.

### Oversized HSTs Cutting

Select the finished size HST you want to make. Cut the background and main square the suggested oversize measurement and trim to the unfinished size. For 4 HSTs you need 2 background and 2 main fabrics.

| FINISHED SIZE | CUT SQUARES | TRIM TO |
|---|---|---|
| 1″ × 1″ | 2¼″ × 2¼″ | 1½″ × 1½″ |
| 1¼″ × 1¼″ | 2½″ × 2½″ | 1¾″ × 1¾″ |
| 1½″ × 1½″ | 2¾″ × 2¾″ | 2″ × 2″ |
| 1¾″ × 1¾″ | 3″ × 3″ | 2¼″ × 2¼″ |
| 2″ × 2″ | 3¼″ × 3¼″ | 2½″ × 2½″ |
| 2¼″ × 2¼″ | 3½″ × 3½″ | 2¾″ × 2¾″ |
| 2½″ × 2½″ | 3¾″ × 3¾″ | 3″ × 3″ |
| 2¾″ × 2¾″ | 4″ × 4″ | 3¼″ × 3¼″ |
| 3″ × 3″ | 4¼″ × 4¼″ | 3½″ × 3½″ |
| 3¼″ × 3¼″ | 4½″ × 4½″ | 3¾″ × 3¾″ |
| 3½″ × 3½″ | 4¾″ × 4¾″ | 4″ × 4″ |

The following example is using 4 HSTs to make a 3½″ × 3½″ Pinwheel block. To follow along, make a copy of the Practice Pinwheel Quilt Block Builder (pullout page P2) and prepare a Quilt Block Base (page 8). Color in the positioning circles to match your colored clips.

### Cutting Squares

*See Precision Cutting (page 31).*

**1.** Cut 2 light and 2 dark 2¾″ × 2¾″ squares.

**2.** Draw a diagonal line on the wrong side of the light squares.

*Note:* If you are working with directional prints, see Using Directional Fabric for Pinwheels (page 70).

## Making HSTs

**1.** Center a light fabric right sides together with a dark fabric.

**2.** To keep the fabric from shifting and stretching along the bias apply small dots of basting glue on the right side of the background fabric, following the direction of the pencil line, about ⅜″ apart. Press to set the glue. Repeat for the remaining block.

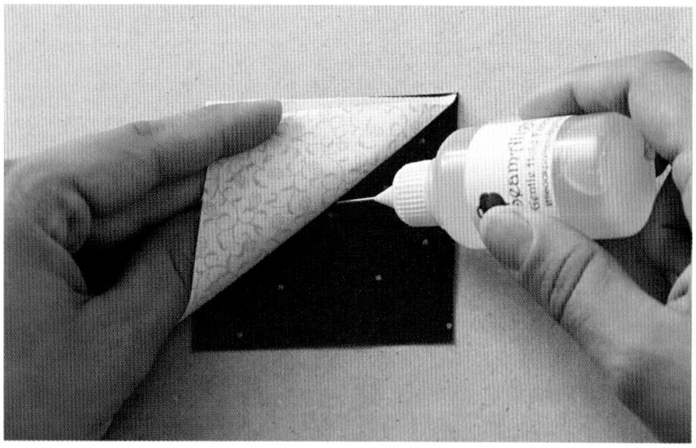

Apply basting glue.

**3.** Stitch ¼″ from one side of the diagonal line.

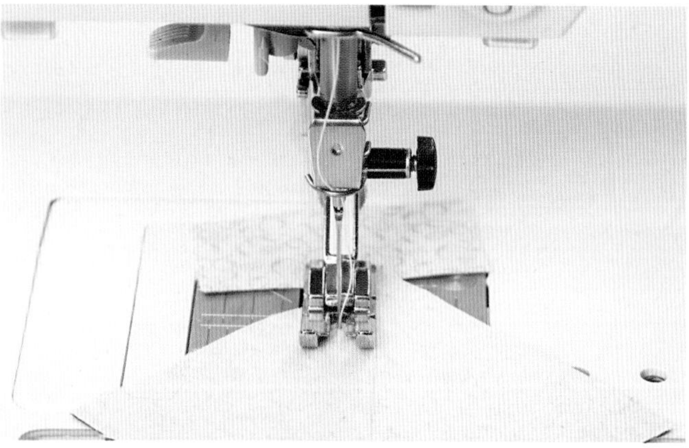

Stitch.

**4.** Remove the block from the machine and clip the threads. Stitch on the opposite side of the diagonal line.

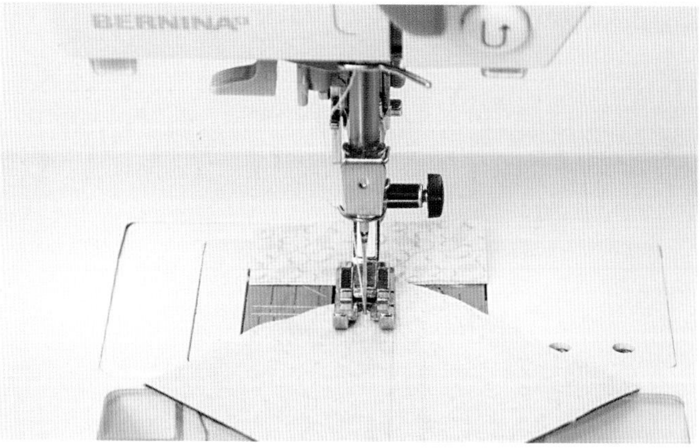

Stitch.

**5.** Cut on the line. Then, trim the seam allowance to 3⁄16″ to help reduce the bulk of the seams. *Do not trim the seams any smaller!*

Cut on the line.

**TIP** If you are making a number of HSTs, this is the perfect time to use chain piecing (page 51).

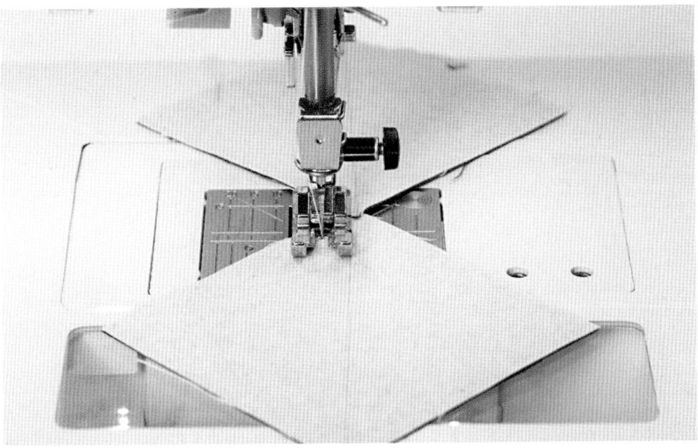

Chain piecing

## Pressing HSTs

Check the Quilt Block Builder for the block you are making and press the seams in the direction indicated by the arrows. In this Pinwheel block, all the seams are pressed toward the dark fabric.

## Trimming

**TIP Accurate Cutting**

- When cutting toward the pressed seam, the fabric tends to move away from the blade, which can result in an inaccurate cut. To avoid this, place a 1″ piece of double-sided tape on your mat. Center the HST right side up on top of the tape and trim. The tape holds the block in position and keeps it from slipping during the trimming process.
- Apply a strip of Tear-Perfect Maker Tape (page 17) along the 45° angle of your ruler. Maker Tape is thick enough that it will lock along the lip of the seam, yet thin enough that it will not compromise the accuracy of the cut. Tear-Perfect Maker Tape will also keep your ruler from slipping while cutting.

Use double-sided tape to keep the block from slipping when trimming.

### *Making the First Vertical Cut*

*Note:* This corner is the most challenging, so cut it first. This way if the cut is off, you can repeat it until it is true.

**1.** Position a HST right side up on the cutting mat with the pressed seam toward you.

**2.** Place the ruler on the HST locking the ridge of tape (see Tips: Accurate Cutting, page 65) along the lip of the seam and leaving about ⅛″ of fabric exposed at the top and to the right of the ruler. Check along the bottom and left side of the HST unit and make sure the fabric is extending beyond the 2″ line both horizontally and vertically.

The amount of fabric extending beyond the edge of the ruler is the amount you will be trimming off the top and right edge of the HST. This has been calculated for in the size of the squares you prepared (see Oversized HSTs Cutting, page 63).

**3.** For a sharp corner, press down with the blade at the top right corner along the right edge and roll the cutter toward you about ½″.

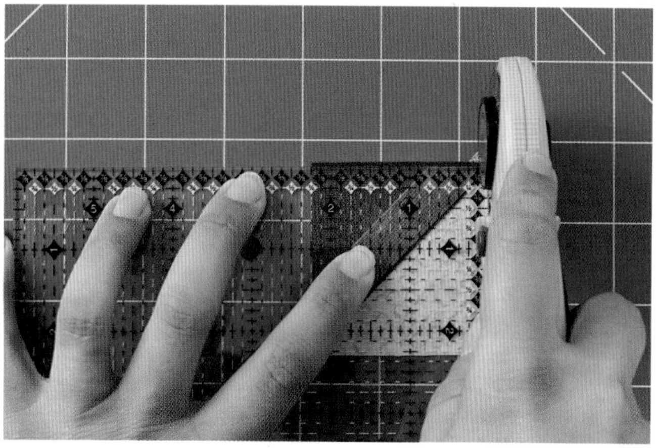

Trim.

**4.** Move the cutter to the bottom right edge of the ruler. Press down with the blade and roll up toward the previous cut to complete the cut.

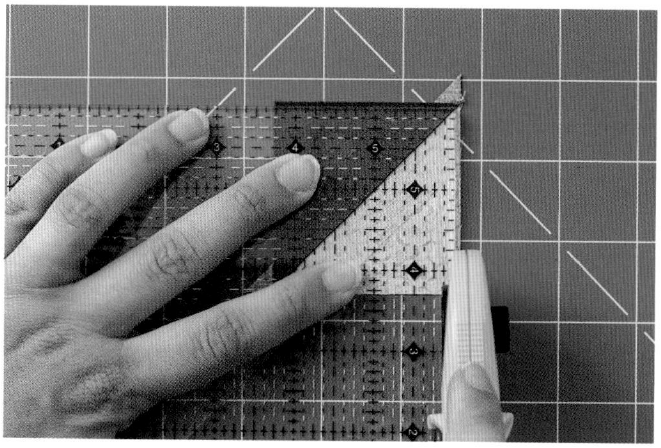

Trim.

### *Making the First Horizontal Cut*

**1.** Place the blade along the top edge of the ruler at the top right corner horizontally.

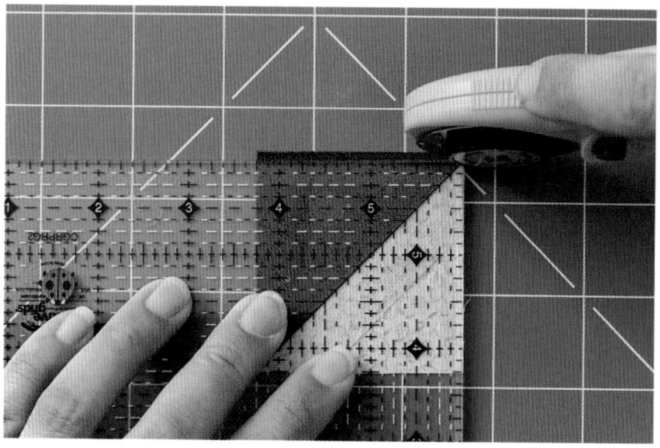

Prepare for trimming.

**2.** Press the blade down and roll to the left to the end of the unit.

*Making the Final Vertical Cut*

**1.** Turn the HST so the edge you just cut is toward you and center the HST on top of the double-sided tape.

**2.** Turn the ruler. Nest the Tear-Perfect Maker Tape along the seam. Line the previously cut edges along the exact line of measure you are cutting the HST to. Line up with the 2″ lines both horizontally and vertically.

**3.** Starting at the top corner, press down with the blade and roll the cutter toward you about ½″.

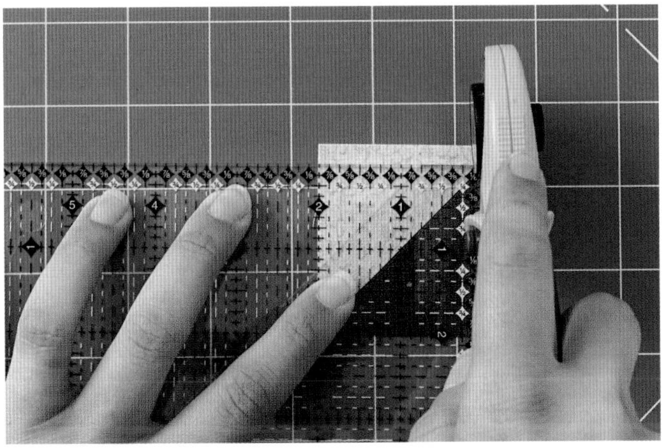

Start cut.

**4.** Move the cutter to the bottom right edge and cut away from you up to the previous cut.

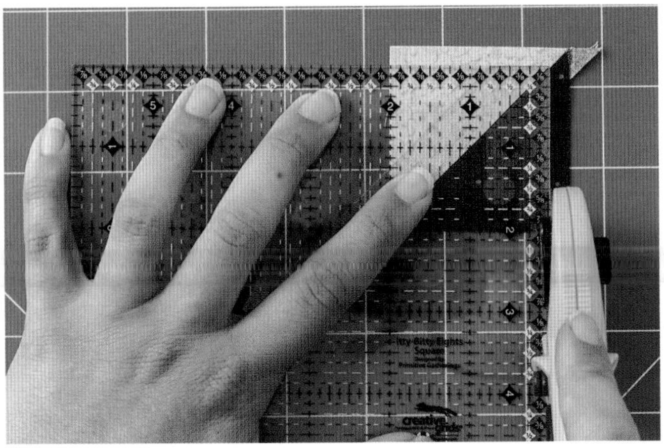

Finish cut.

*Making the Final Horizontal Cut*

**1.** Place the cutter along the top edge horizontally.

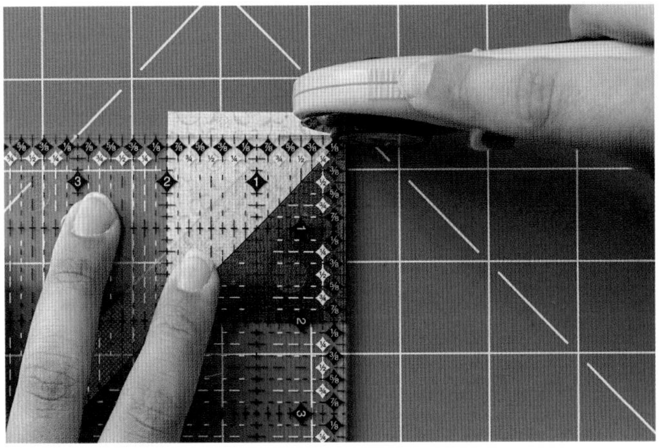

Prepare to cut.

**2.** Press down with the blade in the corner and roll to the left all the way to the end of the unit.

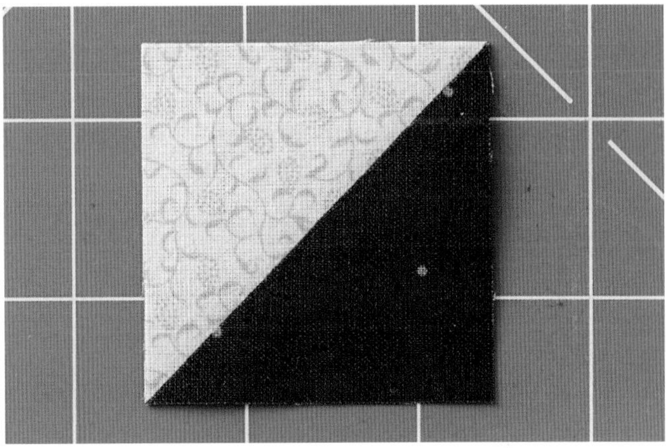

Trimmed block

**3.** Trim all 4 HSTs and place them in position on the Quilt Block Builder.

Trimmed HST units on Quilt Block Builder

## Making Pinwheel Blocks

1. Center the top left and right units, right sides together. Place a dot of basting glue in the corner on the low side of the seam. Nest the diagonal seams and line up the corners. Press to set the glue.

Nest seams

2. Sew the units together and press the seams toward the left.

3. Attach a color-coded clip to the edge and place in position on the Quilt Block Builder.

4. Repeat Steps 1–3 for the bottom left and right HSTs. Attach a color-coded clip on the edge.

Join HSTs and attach clip.

5. Place the 2 units right sides together nesting the center seams.

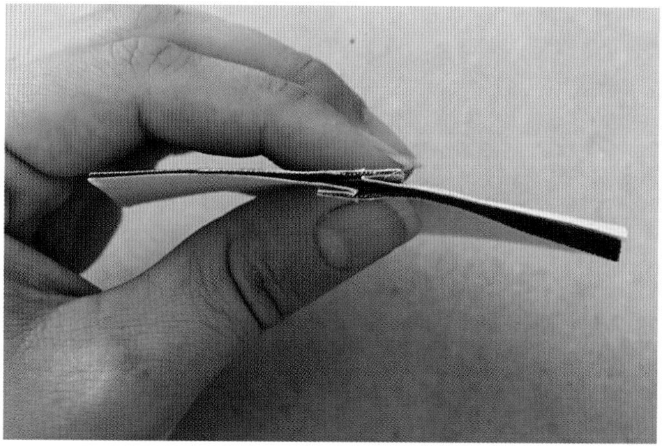

Nest seams.

6. Insert the tip of the basting glue applicator between the 2 pieces. Apply a small dot of glue in the seam allowance along the low side of the seam. Fasten a color-coded clip over the seams.

Apply basting glue.

Fasten a color-coded clip

**7.** Place a drop of basting on one corner. Line up the corners and press to dry. Repeat for the remaining corner.

**8.** Remove the color-coded clip and press.

**9.** Begin stitching. Slow down at the center seam. With eight seams all meeting together in the center it will tend to push to the left. Hold in position with your finger or an awl.

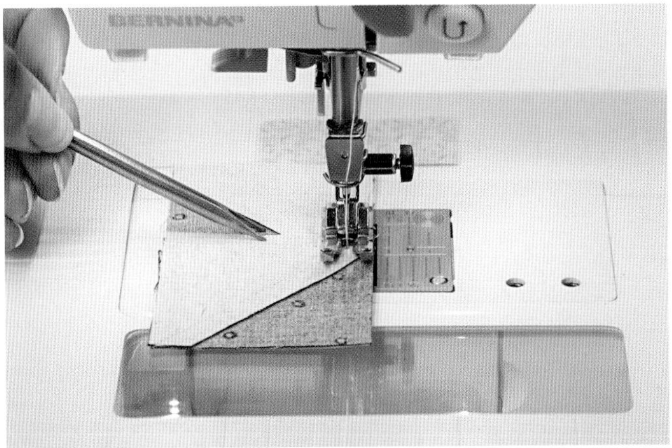

Stitch carefully.

**10.** Fan seams as for the Four-Patch block (see Fanning Seams, page 56). A tiny pinwheel will appear in the center where all the seams meet.

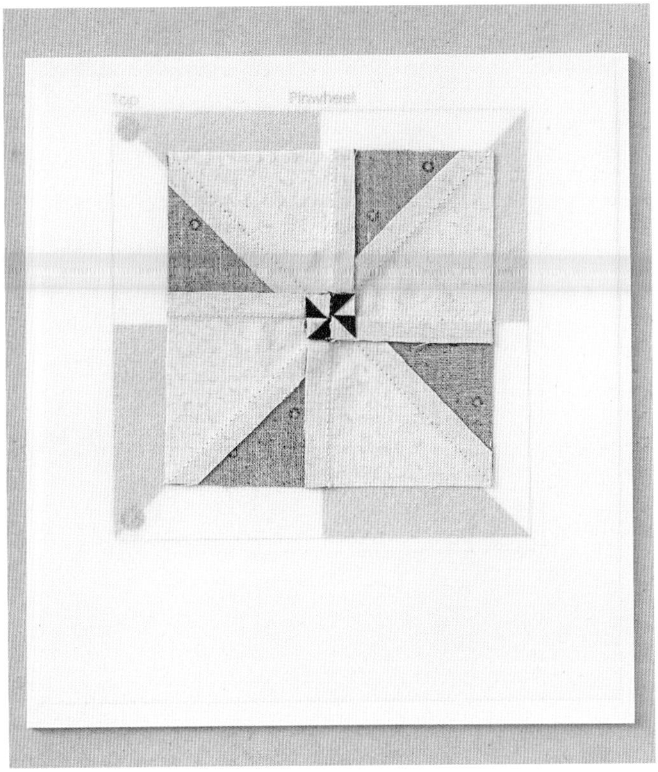

Fan seams.

If your block is does not measure 3½″ × 3½″, now is the time to evaluate where things went wrong. Check your seam allowance and trimming. Fix the mistake and try again.

Pinwheel block on Quilt Block Builder

**NOTE: Pinwheel Precision Piecing**

- *Make sure all the corners match exactly when glue basting, otherwise the eight pieces in the center will not line up.*
- *When glue basting the center of the pinwheel, make sure the HSTs are nested tightly along the seams. If off as much as a thread or two, the center seams will not match.*
- *The center is where all the action is, where all the pieces come together. Before crossing through the center, pause in your stitching. Look where the needle is headed. Make sure it will cross through the X of the seam. Maintain the correct seam allowance. Slow down. Take one stitch at a time through the center.*
- *If the pieces are not matching up check your seams. Did you maintain the same seam allowance for all pieces? Measure. Is one unit too long or too short? Check the seams to see that you have a consistent seam allowance. Maybe increasing or decreasing the seam allowance will make a difference. Being out by a thread or two is magnified when making little blocks.*

# USING DIRECTIONAL FABRIC FOR PINWHEELS

If you use directional prints in your quilts and want the print in the finished block to be facing in the correct direction, use the following failsafe and easy method to get your HSTs started. Once you mark the sewing guidelines, you do not have to think about it again and all the prints will end up in the correct direction.

1. In the pinwheel block, the seams in the top right and the bottom left units run from the top right to the bottom left.

Mark a stitching guideline on the wrong side of the background fabric following the same path.

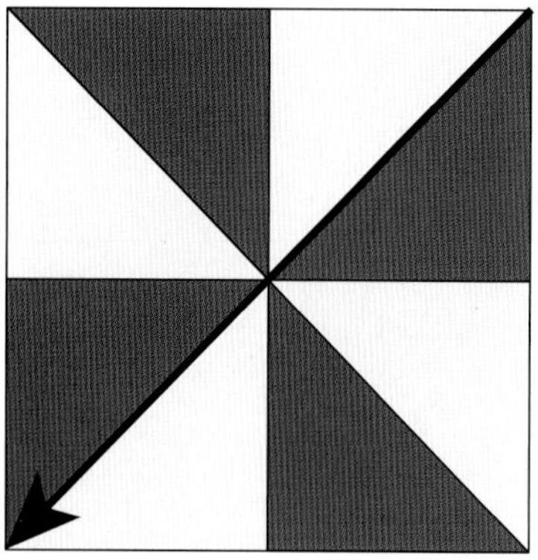

Top right to bottom left

2. The seams of the top left and bottom right units run from the top left to the bottom right.

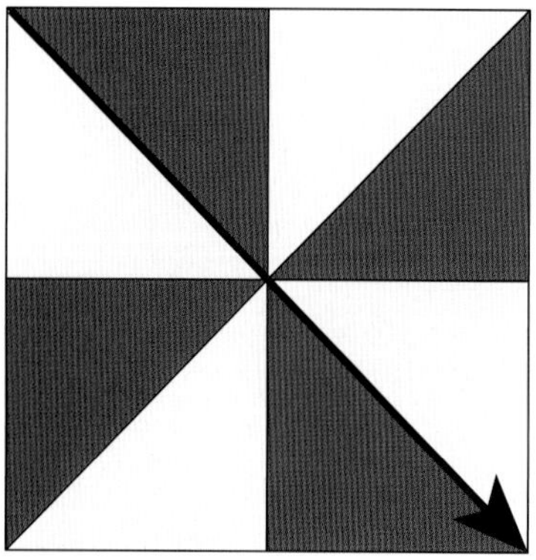

Top left to bottom right

Place the background fabric right side up with the top of the print facing up in the correct direction. Flip the block to the wrong side and mark a dot with a pencil at the top.

## Top Right, Bottom Left

1. Place a main print right side up with the top of the print facing up in the correct direction.

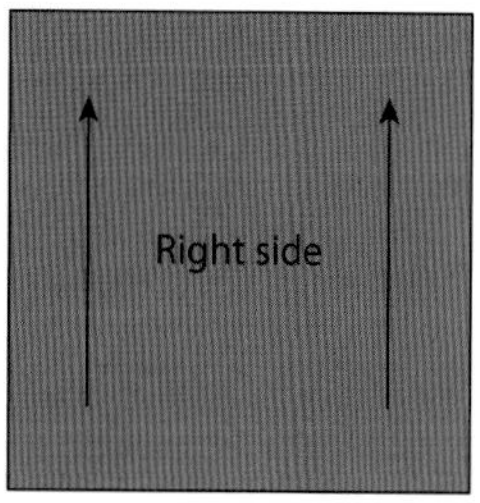


2. Center a background fabric right sides together on top of the main print with the top of the print facing to the right. The pencil dot will be to the right.

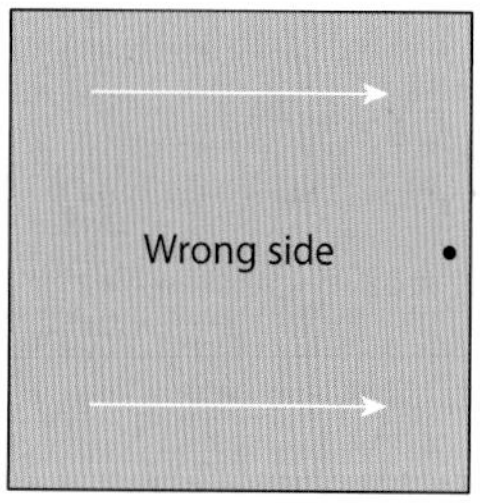


3. Draw a line on the wrong side of the background fabric in the direction of the arrow.

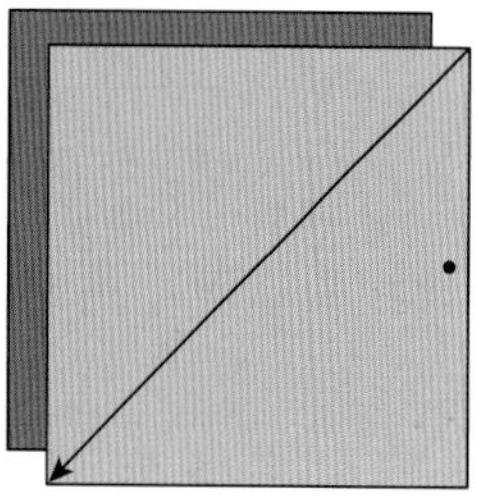

## Top Left, Bottom Right

1. Place a main print right side up with the top of the print facing up in the correct direction.

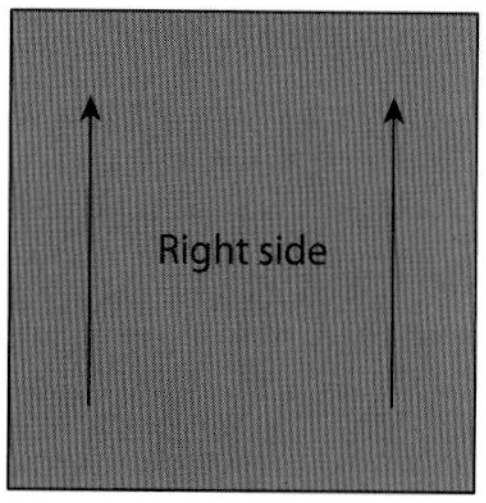


2. Center a background fabric right sides together on top of the main print with the top of the print facing to the left. The pencil dot will be to the left

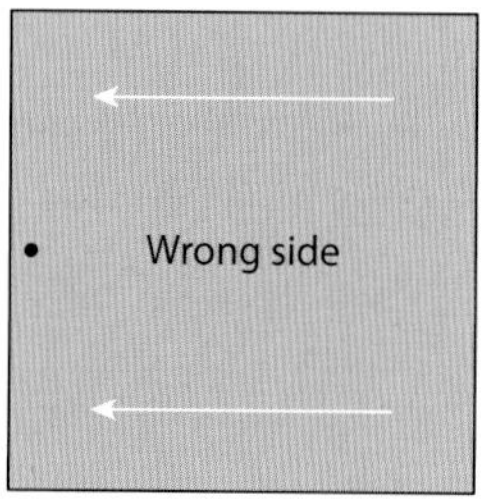


3. Draw a line on the wrong side of the background print in the direction of the arrow.

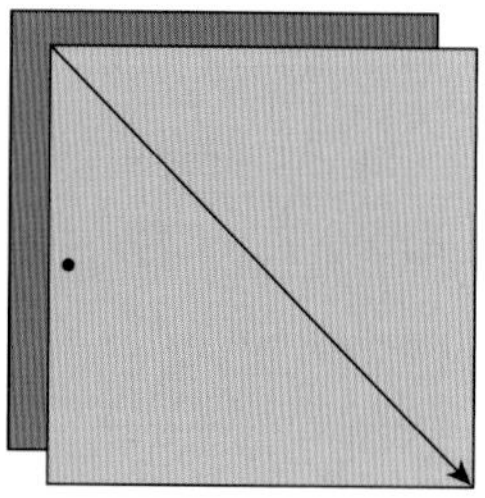

# PINWHEELS AND NINE-PATCHES

**FINISHED QUILT:** 34½″ × 34½″ • **FINISHED BLOCKS:** Framed Pinwheel 6″ × 6″, Nine-Patch 3″ × 3″

Made by Shelley Scott-Tobisch, quilted by Faith McLeod

## FABRIC REQUIREMENTS

*Requirements are based on 40″-wide fabric.*

| PIECE | FABRIC | YARDS |
|---|---|---|
| **A, C, E, sashing** | Light | 1¼ |
| **B, D, F** | Main: all the same or a variety to equal | ½ |
| **Border** | Light | ⅜ |
| **Binding** | Dark | ⅓ |
| **Backing** | Light or main | 1¼ |
| **Batting** | 48″ wide | 1¼ |

## CUTTING

| FABRIC | PIECE | CUT | SIZE | SUBCUT |
|---|---|---|---|---|
| **Light** | A | 2 strips | 3¼″ × WOF | 18 squares 3¼″ × 3¼″ |
| | C | 5 strips | 1½″ × WOF | 36 rectangles 1½″ × 4½″ |
| | E1 | 2 strips | 1½″ × WOF | 32 rectangles 1½″ × 2″ |
| | E2 | 4 strips | 1½″ × WOF | 16 rectangles 1½″ × 4″ |
| | Sashing | 3 strips | 3½″ × WOF | 24 rectangles 3½″ × 6½″ |
| | Borders | 2 strips | 2½″ × WOF | 2 rectangles 2½″ × 30½″ for sides |
| | | 2 strips | 2½″ × WOF | 2 rectangles 2½″ × 34½″ for top and bottom |
| **Main** | B | 2 strips | 3¼″ × WOF | 18 squares 3¼″ × 3¼″ |
| | D | 2 strips | 1½″ × WOF | 36 squares 1½″ × 1½″ |
| | F1 | 1 strips | 1½″ × WOF | 16 rectangles 1½″ × 2″ |
| | F2 | 2 strips | 1½″ × WOF | 32 rectangles 1½″ × 4″ |

## CONSTRUCTION

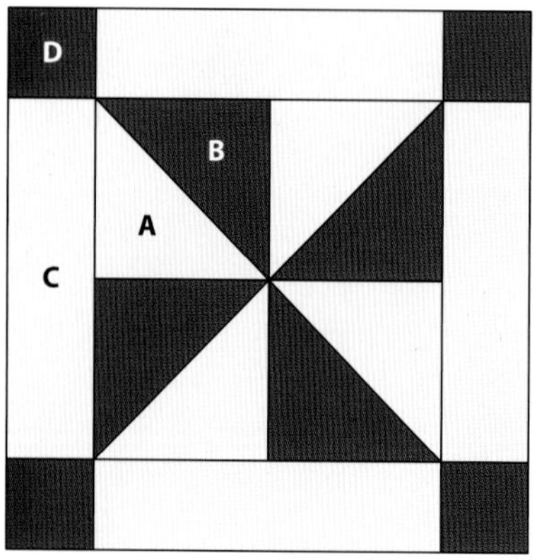


Framed Pinwheel block

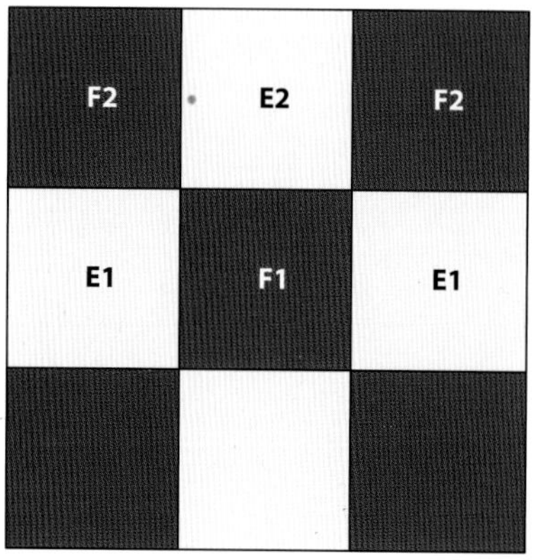


Nine-Patch block

### Block Assembly

*Before you begin, photocopy the Framed Pinwheel Quilt Block Builder (pullout page P2) and Nine-Patch Quilt Block Builder (pullout page P2) and color in the positioning circles to match your clips for color coding (see Positioning Circles, page 10).*

*Piece the Nine-Patch Units*

*See Nine-Patch Block (page 59).*

**1.** Make 16 F/E/F strip sets using E2 and F2 rectangles. Press the seams toward main fabric. Cut 2 strips 1½″ wide from each 4″ strip set.

**2.** Make 16 E/F/E strip sets using E1 and F1 rectangles. Press the seams toward main fabric. Cut 1 strip 1½″ wide from each 2″ strip set.

*Make the Nine-Patch Blocks*

**1.** Make 16 Nine-Patch blocks.

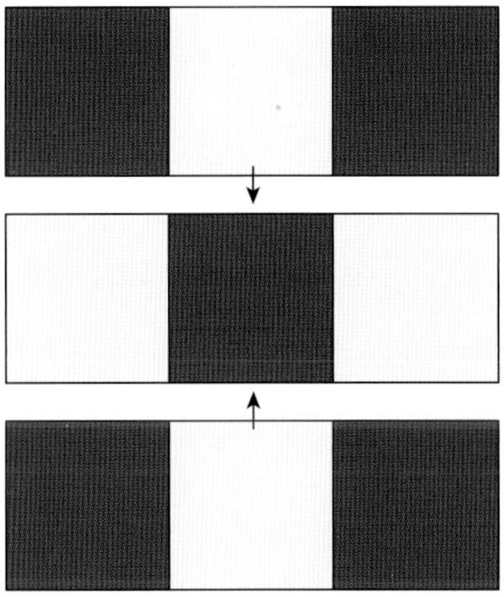

**2.** Make sure the blocks measure 3½″ × 3½″.

*Piece the HST Units*

*See Making HSTs (page 64).*

**1.** Make 36 HSTs from light and main fabric, pieces A and B.

**2.** Press the seams toward the main fabric.

**3.** Trim the HSTs to 2½″ × 2½″.

*Make the Framed Pinwheel Blocks*

*See Making Pinwheel Blocks (page 68).*

**1.** Make 9 Pinwheel blocks.

**2.** Make sure the blocks measure 4½″ × 4½″.

**3.** Sew a C rectangle to the right and left side of each pinwheel.

**TIP** To center the rectangle on the pinwheel, fold the strip in half wrong sides together and pinch the fold on the seam allowance you are sewing to the pinwheel. Line up the crease with the pinwheel seam. Glue the strip in position, and then match and glue the corners. Press to dry. I also use this technique when matching sashing to blocks.

**4.** Sew the main D squares to the right and left short edges of the remaining C rectangles.

**5.** Sew the units to the top and bottom of the pinwheel.

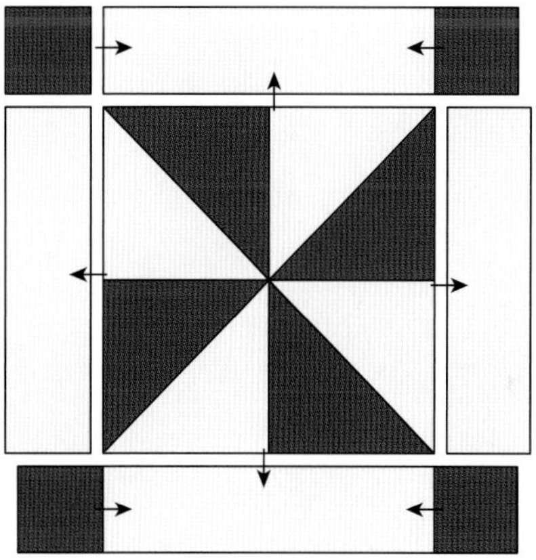

**6.** Make sure the blocks measure 6½″ × 6½″ (including seam allowances).

## Assemble the Quilt

1. Make 4 rows of nine-patches and sashing.

2. Make 3 rows of framed pinwheels and sashing.

3. Sew the rows together.

4. Add the side borders, then the top and bottom borders (see Borders, page 96).

## Finish the Quilt

1. Layer the top, batting, and backing (see Backing, page 98) and quilt as desired.

2. Bind and label (see Binding, page 98).

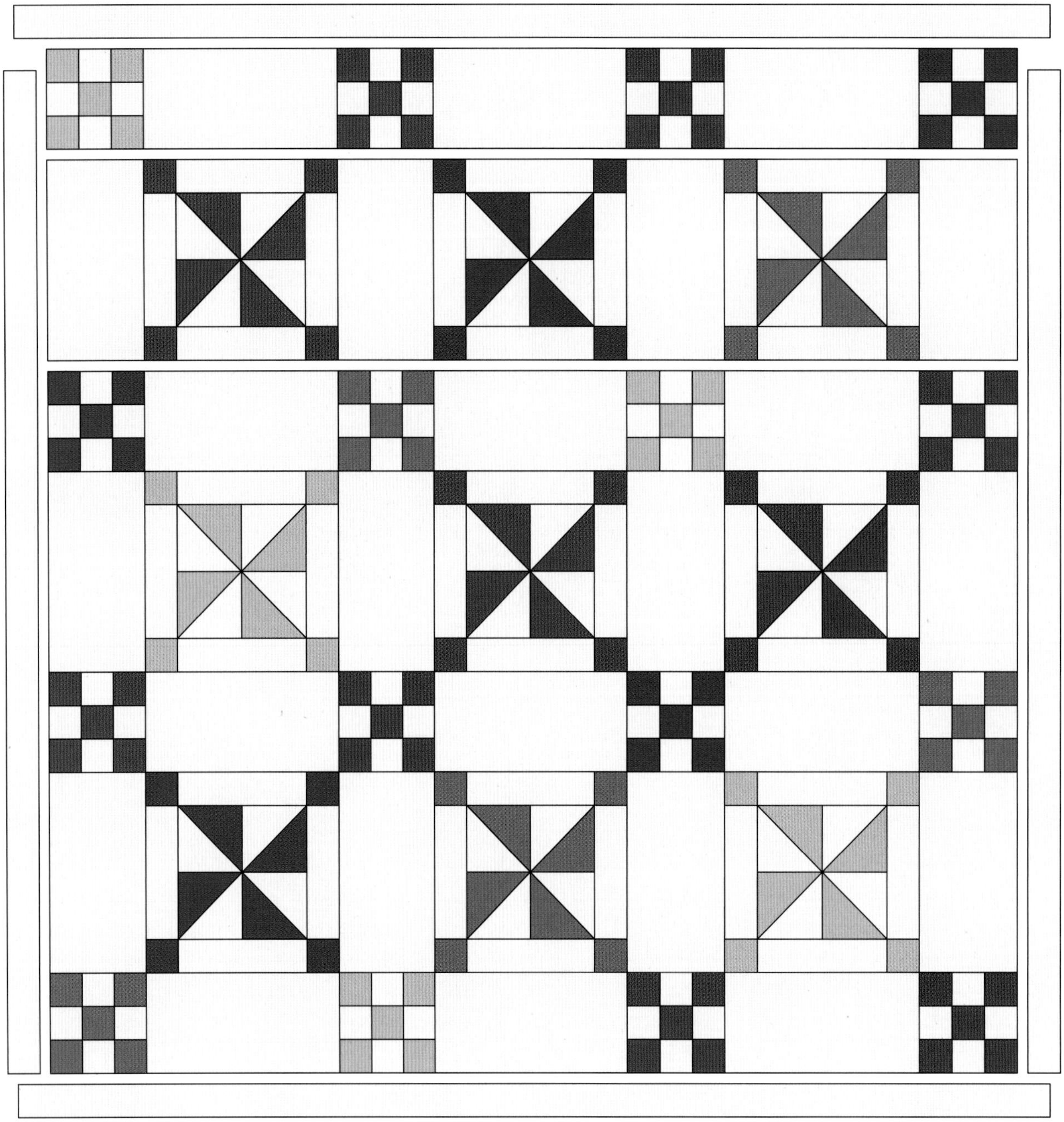

Quilt assembly

# SAWMILL BAY

**FINISHED QUILT:** 45½″ × 45½″ • **FINISHED BLOCK:** Sawmill 10″ × 10″

Made by Patricia Haslop, quilted by Lauren Tolhurst

## FABRIC REQUIREMENTS

*Requirements are based on 40″-wide fabric.*

| PIECE | FABRIC | YARDS |
|---|---|---|
| **A, C, sashing** | Light | 2¼ |
| **B** | Main 1: all the same or a variety to equal | ⅝ |
| **D** | Main 2: all the same or a variety to equal | 1⅛ |
| **Cornerstones** | Main 1 | ⅛ |
| **Binding** | Main 2 | ⅓ |
| **Backing** | Light, main, or pieced to equal | 3 |
| **Batting** | 90″ wide | 1½ |

## CUTTING

| FABRIC | PIECE | CUT | SIZE | SUBCUT |
|---|---|---|---|---|
| **Light** | A | 4 strips | 4¼″ × WOF | 32 squares 4¼″ × 4¼″ |
| | C | 11 strips | 3¼″ × WOF | 128 squares 3¼″ × 3¼″ |
| | Sashing | 2 strips | 10½″ × WOF | 40 rectangles 10½″ × 1½″ |
| **Main 1** | B | 4 strips | 4¼″ × WOF | 32 squares 4¼″ × 4¼″ |
| | Cornerstones | 1 strip | 1½″ × WOF | 25 squares 1½″ × 1½″ |
| **Main 2** | D | 11 strips | 3¼″ × WOF | 128 squares 3¼″ × 3¼″ |

## CONSTRUCTION

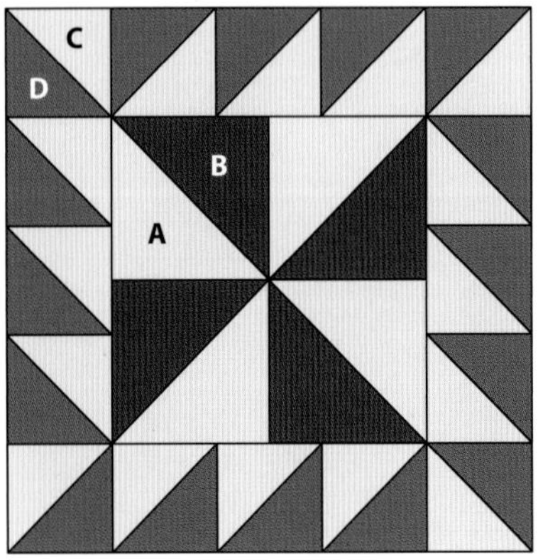


Sawmill block

### Block Assembly

*Before you begin, photocopy the Sawmill Bay Quilt Block Builder (pullout page P1) and color in the positioning circles to match your clips for color coding (see Positioning Circles, page 10).*

*Piece HST Units A and B*

*See Making HSTs (page 64).*

**1.** Make 64 HSTs from pieces A and B.

**2.** Press the seams toward the main fabric.

**3.** Trim the HSTs to 3½″ × 3½″.

*Piece HST Units C and D*

**1.** Make 256 HSTs from pieces C and D.

**2.** Press the seams toward the main fabric.

**3.** Trim the HSTs to 2½″ × 2½″.

*Make the Pinwheels*

*See Making Pinwheel Blocks (page 68).*

**1.** Make 16 pinwheels with the A/B HSTs.

**2.** Make sure the blocks measure 6½″ × 6½″ square.

*Assemble the Blocks*

Piece 16 Sawmill blocks. Make sure the blocks measure 10½″ × 10½″ (including seam allowances).

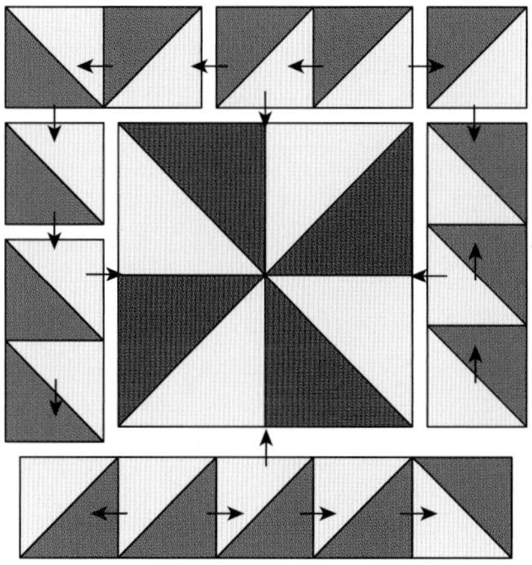

## Assemble the Quilt

**1.** Make 4 rows of Sawmill blocks and sashing.

**2.** Make 5 rows of sashing and cornerstones.

**3.** Sew the rows together.

## Finish the Quilt

**1.** Layer the top, batting, and backing (see Backing, page 98) and quilt as desired.

**2.** Bind and label (see Binding, page 98).

Quilt assembly

# PLUM PUDDING

**FINISHED QUILT:** 64½″ × 80½″ • **FINISHED BLOCK:** Cobblestones 8″ × 8″

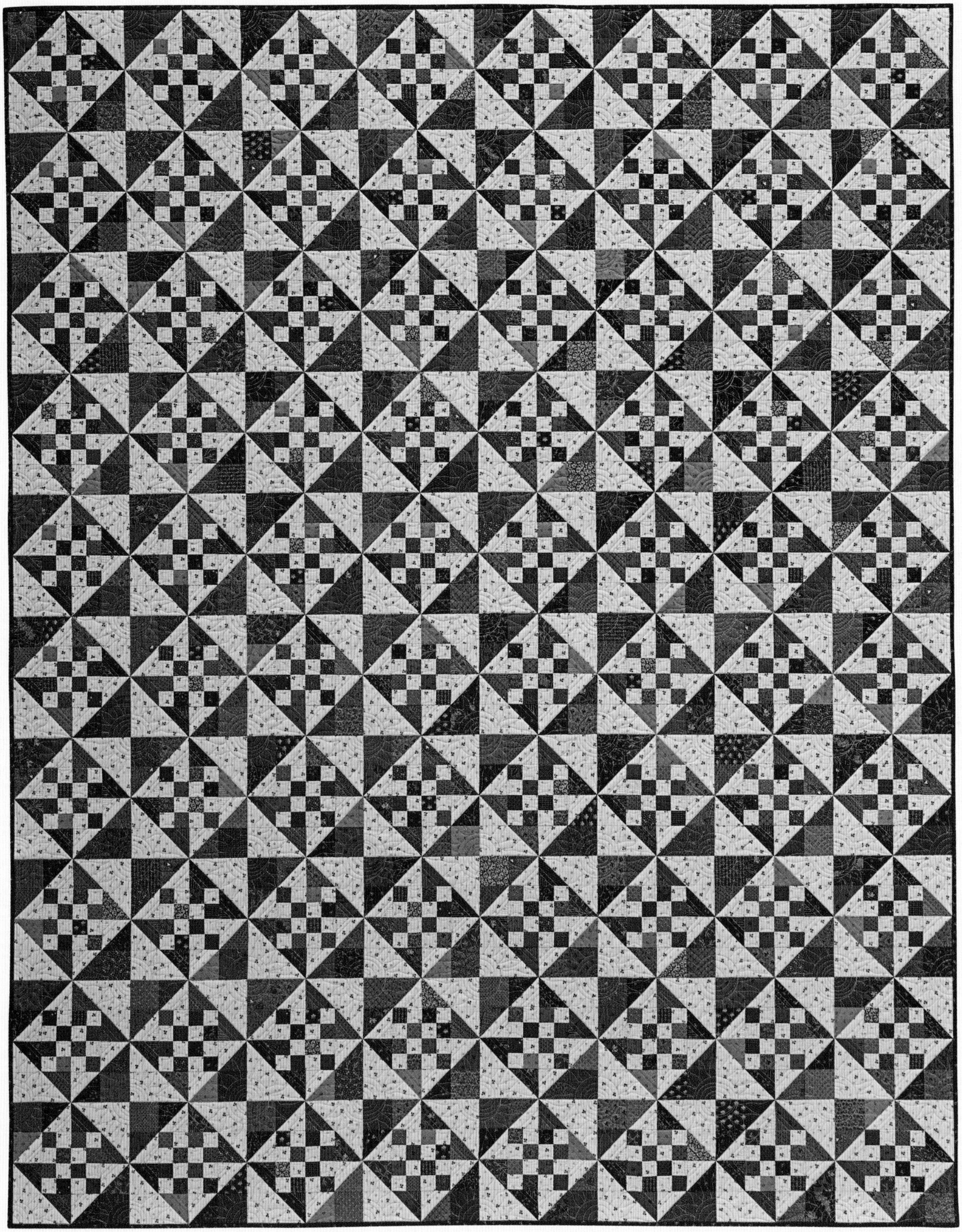

Made by Carrie Lakatos, quilted by Faith Mcleod

## FABRIC REQUIREMENTS

*Requirements are based on 40″-wide fabric.*

| PIECE | FABRIC | YARDS |
|---|---|---|
| **A, B, E** | Main: all the same or a variety to equal | 4½ |
| **C, D, F** | Light | 4½ |
| **Binding** | Dark | ½ |
| **Backing** | Light or main | 5 |
| **Batting** | 90″ wide | 2 |

## CUTTING

| FABRIC | PIECE | CUT | SIZE | SUBCUT |
|---|---|---|---|---|
| **Light** | C | 27 strips | 3¼″ × WOF | 320 squares 3¼″ × 3¼″ |
| | D | 10 strips | 2½″ × WOF | 160 squares 2½″ × 2½″ |
| | F | 25 strips | 1½″ × WOF | 50 strips 1½″ × 20″ |
| **Main** | A | 10 strips | 2½″ × WOF | 160 squares 2½″ × 2½″ |
| | B | 27 strips | 3¼″ × WOF | 320 squares 3¼″ × 3¼″ |
| | E | 25 strips | 1½″ × WOF | 50 strips 1½″ × 20″ |

## CONSTRUCTION

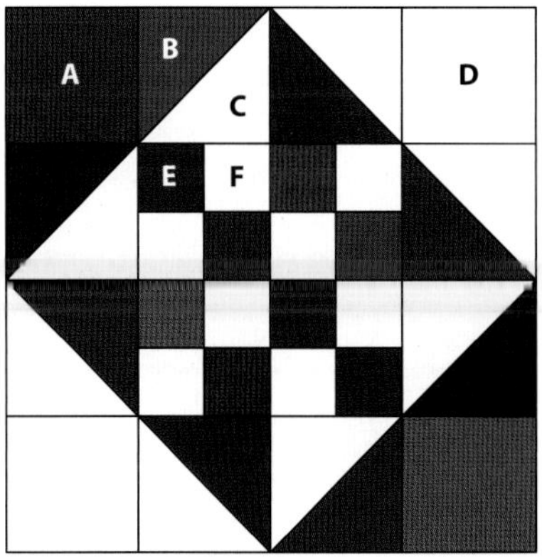

Cobblestones block

### Block Assembly

*Before you begin, photocopy the Cobblestones Quilt Block Builder (pullout page P2) and color in the positioning circles to match your clips for color coding (see Positioning Circles, page 10).*

*Piece the HST Units*

*See Making HSTs (page 64)*

**1.** Make 640 HSTs from pieces B and C.

**2.** Press the seams toward the main fabric.

**3.** Trim the HSTs to 2½″ × 2½″.

### *Piece the Sixteen-Patch Units*

The shorter 20″ strips are easier to work with. They will remain straighter when sewing, pressing, and subcutting.

**1.** Make 32 E/F/E/F strip sets 20″ × 4½″. Press the seams toward the *light* fabric.

**2.** Subcut into 320 strips 1½″ × 4½″.

For a scrappy quilt, add variety to the blocks by creating several different strip set combinations.

**4.** Arrange 4 strips as shown.

**5.** Sew strips together in sets of 2.

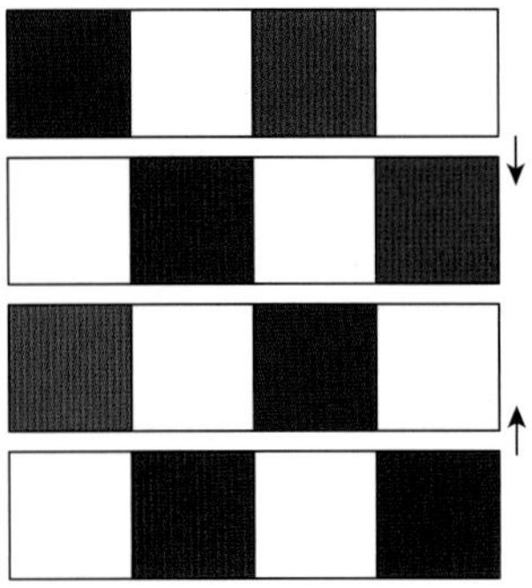

**6.** Sew sets of 2 strips together and fan the center seams (see Fanning Seams, page 56).

× = Fan seams

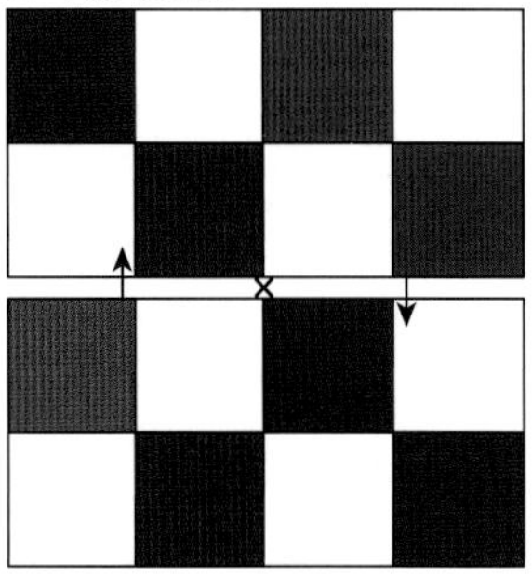

**7.** Make sure the units measure 4½″ × 4½″ (including seam allowances).

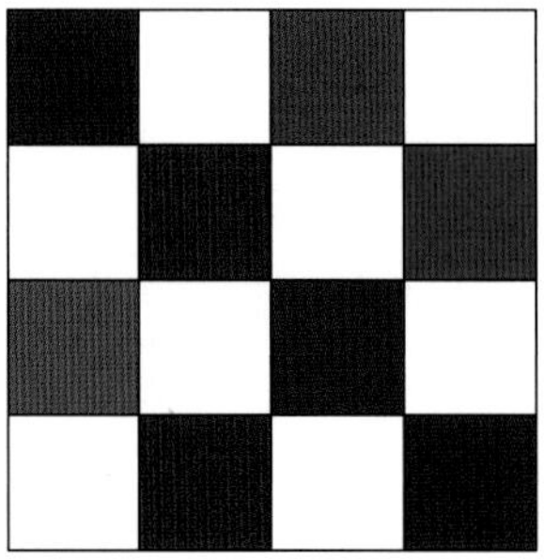

### *Make the Cobblestone Blocks*

Piece 80 Cobblestone blocks. Make sure the blocks measure 8½″ × 8½″ (including seam allowances).

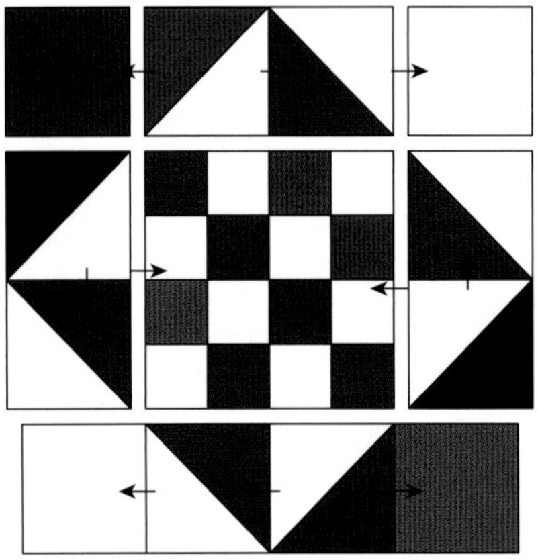

## Assemble the Quilt

*See Pieced Borders (page 96).*

1. Make 10 rows of 8 Cobblestone blocks. Fan the pinwheel seams between the blocks to ease bulk (see Fanning Seams, page 56).

2. Sew the rows together.

## Finish the Quilt

1. Layer the top, batting, and backing (see Backing, page 98) and quilt as desired.

2. Bind and label (see Binding, page 98).

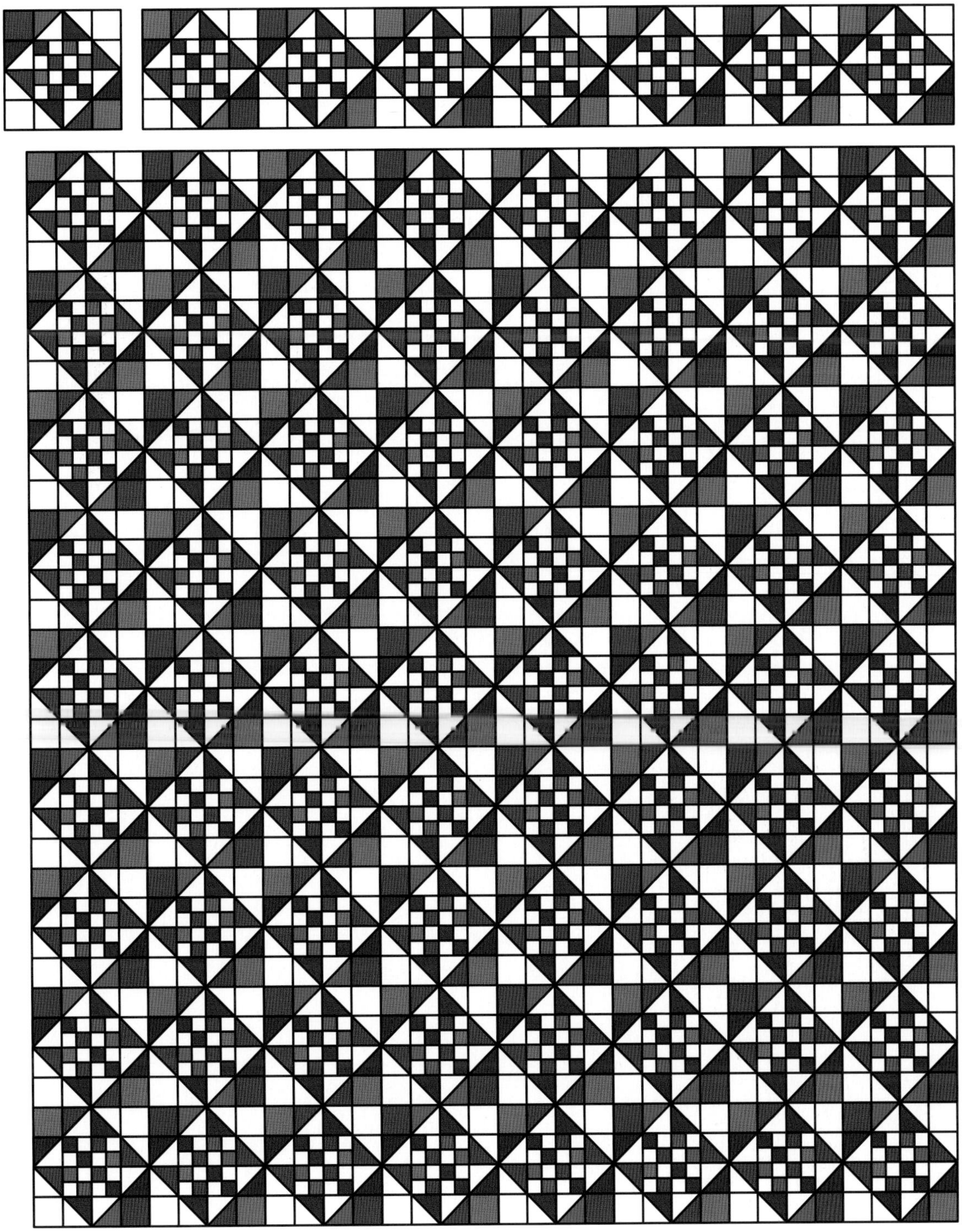

Quilt assembly

# SONG OF FRIENDSHIP

**FINISHED QUILT:** 51½″ × 63½″ • **FINISHED BLOCK:** Delectable Mountains 6″ × 6″

Made by Carrie Lakatos, quilted by Faith McLeod

## FABRIC REQUIREMENTS

*Requirements are based on 40″-wide fabric.*

| PIECE | FABRIC | YARDS |
|---|---|---|
| **A, B, F, border HSTs, border** | Light | 3½ |
| **C** | Main 1: all the same or a variety to equal | 1 |
| **D, E, border HSTs** | Main 2: all the same or a variety to equal | 1½ |
| **Binding** | Dark | ½ |
| **Backing** | Dark, main, or pieced to equal | 3⅜ |
| **Batting** | 90″ wide | 1¾ |

## CUTTING

*Cut strips from selvage to selvage.*

| FABRIC | PIECE | CUT | SIZE | SUBCUT |
|---|---|---|---|---|
| **Light** | A | 4 strips | 2″ × WOF | 80 squares 2″ × 2″ |
| | B | 12 strips | 2¾″ × WOF | 160 squares 2¾″ × 2¾″ |
| | F | 8 strips | 6⅞″ × WOF | 40 squares 6⅞″ × 6⅞″; subcut diagonally once |
| | Border HSTs | 2 strips | 2¾″ × WOF | 20 squares 2¾″ × 2¾″ |
| | Border | 5 strips | 2″ × WOF | 18 rectangles 2″ × 9½″ |
| **Main 1** | C | 12 strips | 2¾″ × WOF | 160 squares 2¾″ × 2¾″ |
| **Main 2** | D | 4 strips | 3⅞″ × WOF | 40 squares 3⅞″ × 3⅞″; subcut diagonally once |
| | E | 5 strips | 2⅜″ × WOF | 80 squares 2⅜″ × 2⅜″; subcut diagonally once |
| | Border HSTs | 2 strips | 2¾″ × WOF | 20 squares 2¾″ × 2¾″ |

## CONSTRUCTION

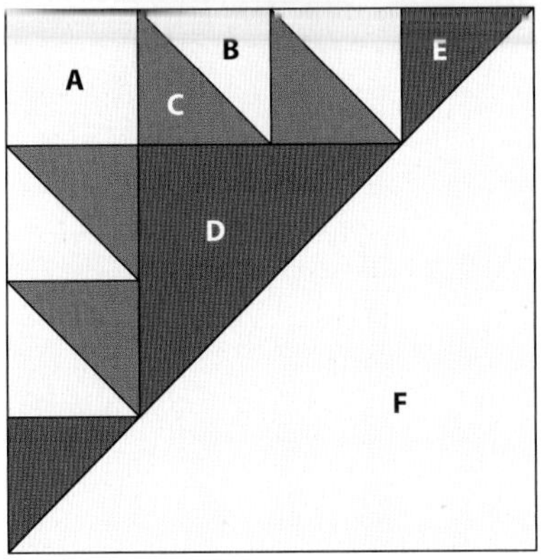


Delectable Mountains block

### Block Assembly

*Before you begin, photocopy the Delectable Mountains Quilt Block Builder (pullout page P2) and color in the positioning circles to match your clips for color coding (see Positioning Circles, page 10).*

*Piece the HST Units*

*See Making HSTs (page 64).*

1. Make 320 HSTs from pieces B and C.

2. Make 40 HSTs from light and main 2 squares for the border pinwheels.

3. Press the seams toward the main fabric.

4. Trim the HSTs to 2″ × 2″.

*Make the Song of Friendship Blocks*

**1.** Piece 80 Delectable Mountains blocks.

**2.** Make sure the blocks measure 6½″ × 6½″ (including seam allowances).

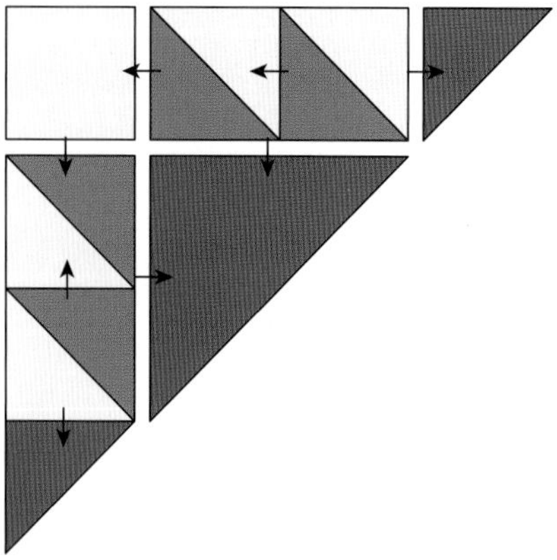

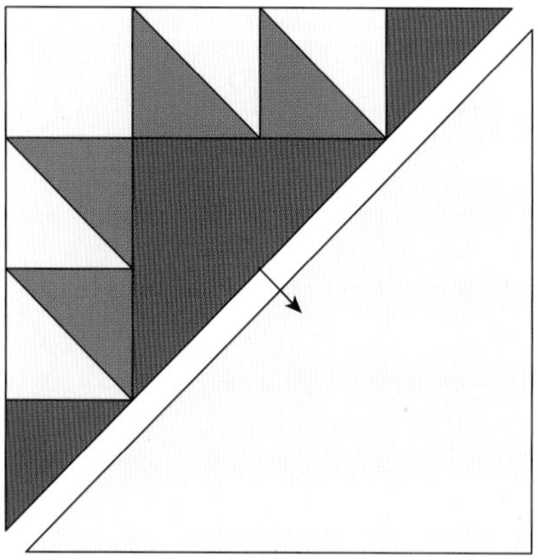

**3.** Join the blocks together in groups of 4 (see Note: Pinwheel Precision Piecing, page 69).

**4.** Fan the pinwheel seams between the blocks to ease the bulk (see Fanning Seams, page 56).

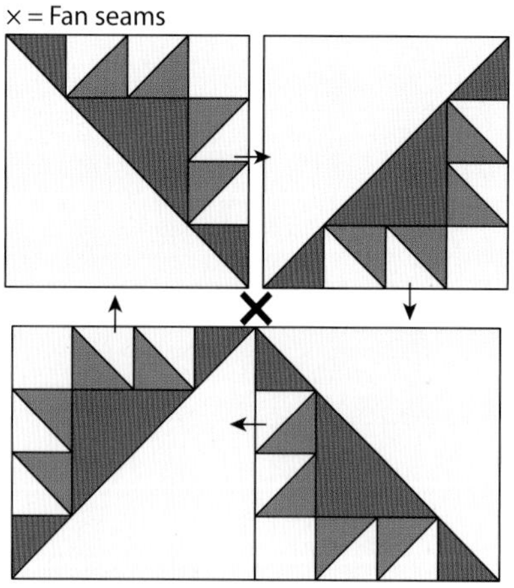

## Assemble the Quilt

*See Pieced Borders (page 96).*

**1.** Make 5 rows of 4 blocks.

**2.** Sew the rows together.

*Make the Borders*

**1.** Sew an HST to both short ends of a 2″ × 9½″ border strip, noting the orientation.

**2.** Press the seams toward the border strip. Make 18.

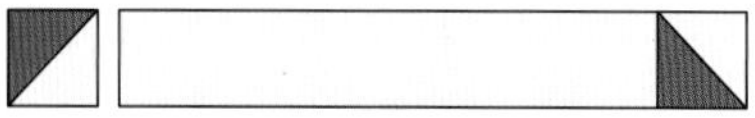

*Make the Side Borders*

Sew 2 sets of 5 border strips.

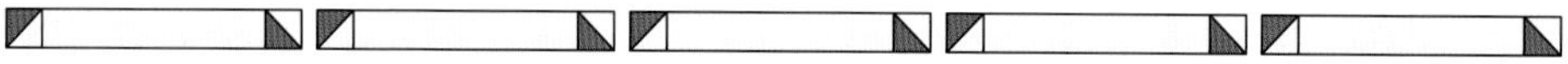

*Make the Top and Bottom Borders*

**1.** Sew 2 sets of 4 border strips.

**2.** Sew an HST to each end of the 4 border strips.

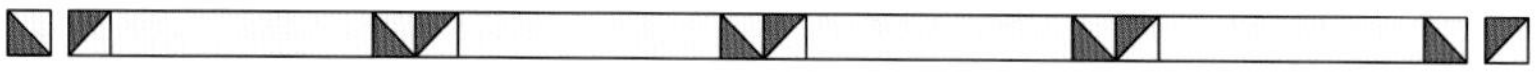

*Sew the Borders to the Quilt*

Add the side borders, then the top and bottom borders.

## Finish the Quilt

1. Layer the top, batting, and backing (see Backing, page 98) and quilt as desired.

2. Bind and add label (see Binding, page 98).

Quilt assembly

# MUSKRAT HOLLOW

**FINISHED QUILT:** 61½″ × 72″ • **FINISHED BLOCK:** Muskrat Paw 9″ × 9″

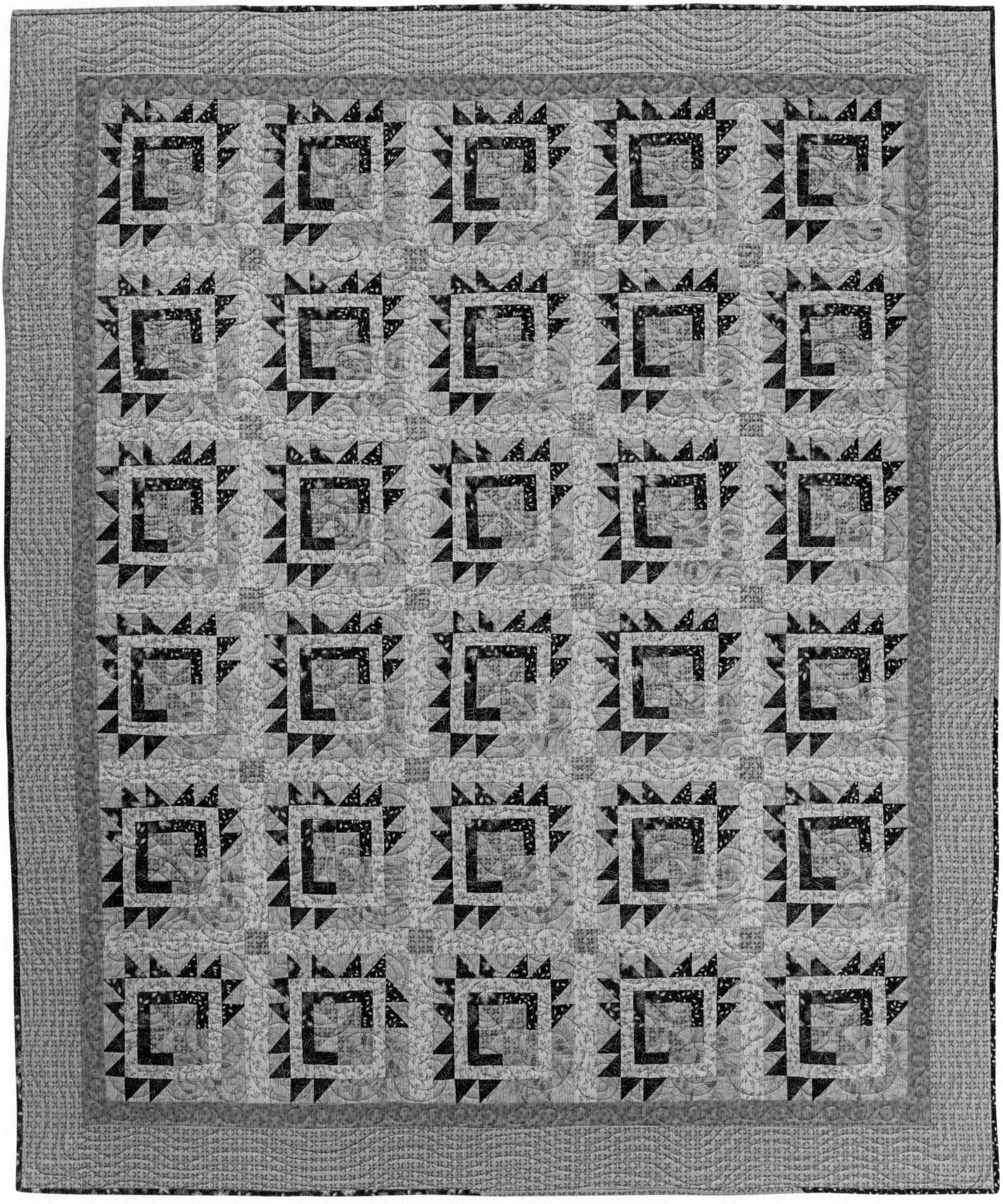

Made by Ione MacLennan, quilted by Lauren Tolhurst

## FABRIC REQUIREMENTS

*Requirements are based on 40″-wide fabric.*

| PIECE | FABRIC | YARDS |
|---|---|---|
| **A, B, E** | Light 1 | 2¾ |
| **C1, F1, G1** | Main 1 | ⅝ |
| **C2, F2, G2** | Main 2 | ⅝ |
| **C3, F3, G3** | Main 3 | ⅝ |
| **C4, F4, G4** | Main 4 | ⅝ |
| **D** | Main 5 | ½ |
| **H, I** | Light 2 | ⅞ |
| **Sashing** | Light 2 | 1 |
| **Cornerstones** | Main 5 | ⅛ |
| **Border 1** | Main 5 | ½ |
| **Border 2** | Light 1 | 1 |
| **Binding** | Main 5 | ½ |
| **Backing** | Light or main | 4 |
| **Batting** | 90″ wide | 2 |

*Note: Yardage for blocks, sashing, borders, and so on are listed separately. When shopping or stash busting, label each fabric to avoid confusion later.*

## CUTTING

| FABRIC | PIECE | CUT | SIZE | SUBCUT |
|---|---|---|---|---|
| **Light 1** | A | 6 strips | 2″ × WOF | 120 squares 2″ × 2″ |
| | B | 22 strips | 2¾″ × WOF | 240 squares 2¾″ × 2¾″ |
| | E | 5 strips | 2¾″ × WOF | 60 squares 2¾″ × 2¾″ |
| | Border 2 | 4 strips | 4″ × WOF | 2 strips 4″ × 65″ for sides |
| | | 4 strips | 4″ × WOF | 2 strips 4″ × 61½″ for top and bottom |
| **Light 2** | H | 2 strips | 5″ × WOF | 60 rectangles 5″ × 1¼″ |
| | I | 2 strips | 6½″ × WOF | 60 rectangles 6½″ × 1¼″ |
| | Sashing | 3 strips | 9½″ × WOF | 49 rectangles 9½″ × 2″ |
| **Main 1–4** | C1–C4 | 5 strips | 2¾″ × WOF | 60 squares 2¾″ × 2¾″ |
| | F1–F4 | 1 strip | 2″ × WOF | 30 rectangles 2″ × 1¼″ |
| | G1–G4 | 1 strip | 2¾″ × WOF | 30 rectangles 2¾″ × 1¼″ |
| **Main 5** | D | 5 strips | 2¾″ × WOF | 60 squares 2¾″ × 2¾″ |
| | Cornerstones | 1 strip | 2″ × WOF | 20 squares 2″ × 2″ |
| | Border 1 | 4 strips | 2″ × WOF | 2 strips 2″ × 62″ for sides |
| | | 3 strips | 2″ × WOF | 2 strips 2″ × 54½″ for top and bottom |

## CONSTRUCTION

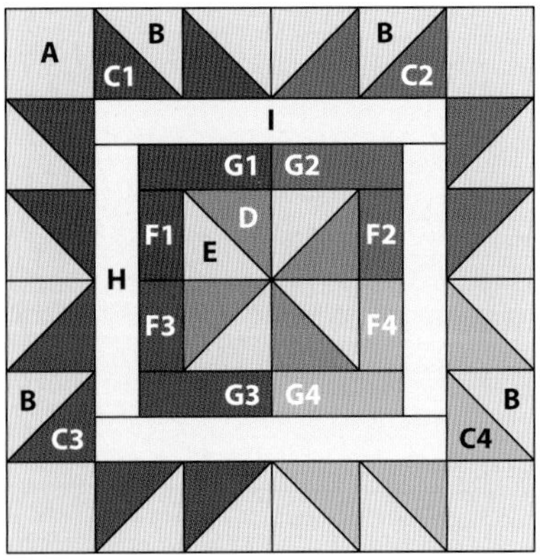


Muskrat Paw block

### Block Assembly

*Before you begin, photocopy the Muskrat Paw Quilt Block Builder (pullout page P1) and color in the positioning circles to match your clips for color coding (see Positioning Circles, page 10).*

#### *Piece the HST Units*

*See Making HSTs (page 64).*

1. Make 120 HSTs from pieces B and C1.
2. Make 120 HSTs from pieces B and C2.
3. Make 120 HSTs from pieces B and C3.
4. Make 120 HSTs from pieces B and C4.
5. Make 120 HSTs from pieces E and D.
6. Trim the HSTs to 2″ × 2″.

*Note:* Be sure to refer to the Muskrat Paw Quilt Block Builder to see which direction to press the seams. Some HSTs are pressed to the light fabric and some are pressed to the main fabric. HSTs in the Muskrat Paw block have nesting seams and need to oppose for best results.

#### *Make the Pinwheel Center*

*See Making Pinwheel Blocks (page 68).*

1. Make 30 pinwheels with HSTs from Piece the HST Units, Step 5 (column at left).
2. Make sure Pinwheel blocks measure 3½″ × 3½″.
3. Sew an F1 rectangle to an F3 rectangle and an F2 rectangle to an F4 rectangle along the short edges.
4. Sew an F1/F3 unit to the left of the pinwheel and an F2/F4 unit to the right of the pinwheel.
5. Sew a G1 rectangle to a G2 rectangle and a G3 rectangle to a G4 rectangle along the short edges.
6. Sew a G1/G2 unit to the top of the pinwheel and a G3/G4 unit to the bottom of the pinwheel. Press the seams toward the outer units.

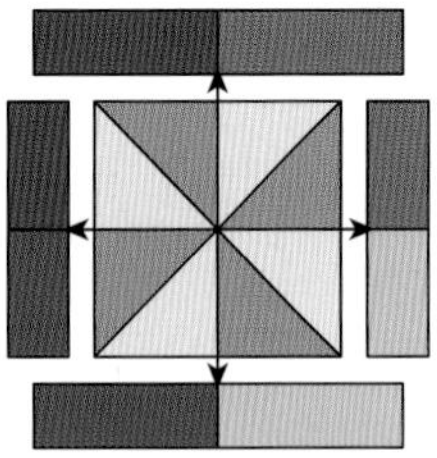

7. Sew an H rectangle to the left and right side. Press seams toward the outer strips.
8. Sew an I rectangle to the top and bottom. Press seams toward the outer strips.

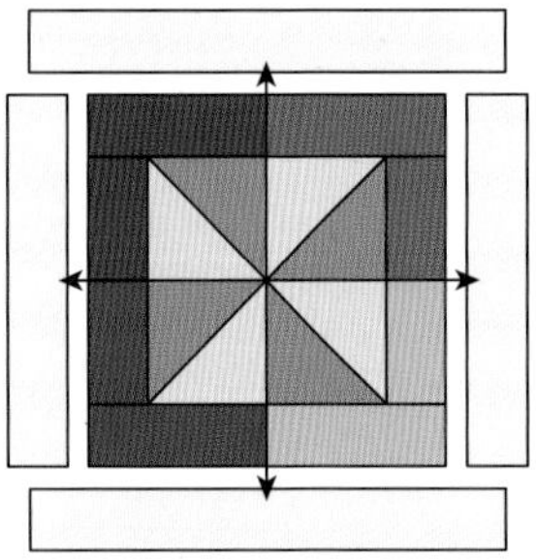

#### *Make the Paws*

1. Sew the HSTs together in groups of 2.

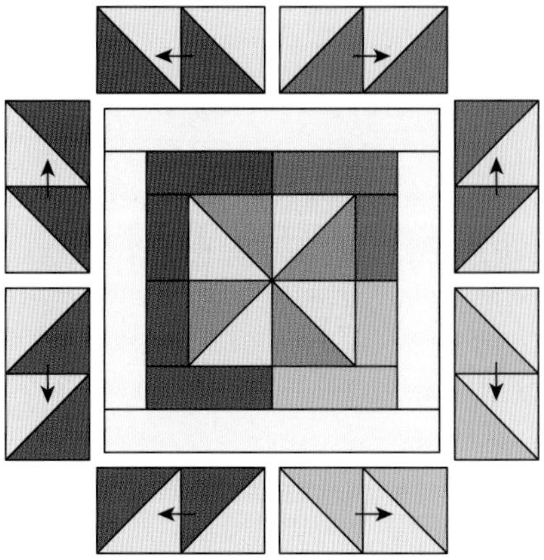

2. Assemble the block.

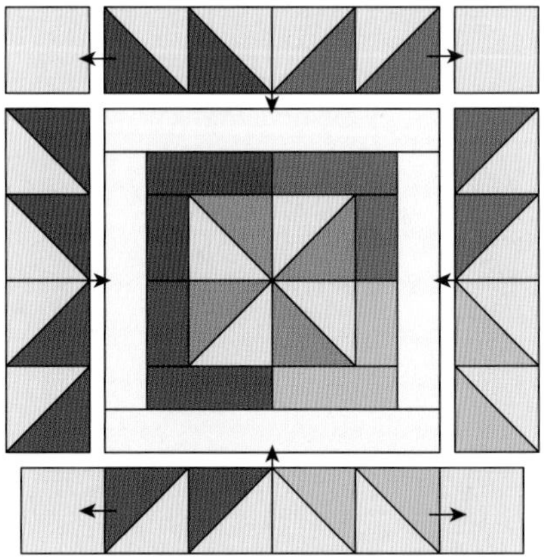

3. Make sure the blocks measure 9½″ × 9½″.

## Assemble the Quilt

1. Make 6 rows of 5 Muskrat Paw blocks and sashing.

2. Make 5 rows of sashing and cornerstones.

3. Sew the rows together.

4. Add border 1 to the left and right sides, and then add the top and bottom (see Borders, page 96).

5. Add border 2 to the left and right sides, and then add the top and bottom.

## Finish the Quilt

1. Layer the top, batting, and backing (see Backing, page 98) and quilt as desired.

2. Bind and label (see Binding, page 98).

Quilt assembly

# APPLEYARD LANE

**FINISHED QUILT:** 51½″ × 60″ • **FINISHED BLOCKS:** Shoo Fly 3″ × 3″, Double Four-Patch 3″ × 3″

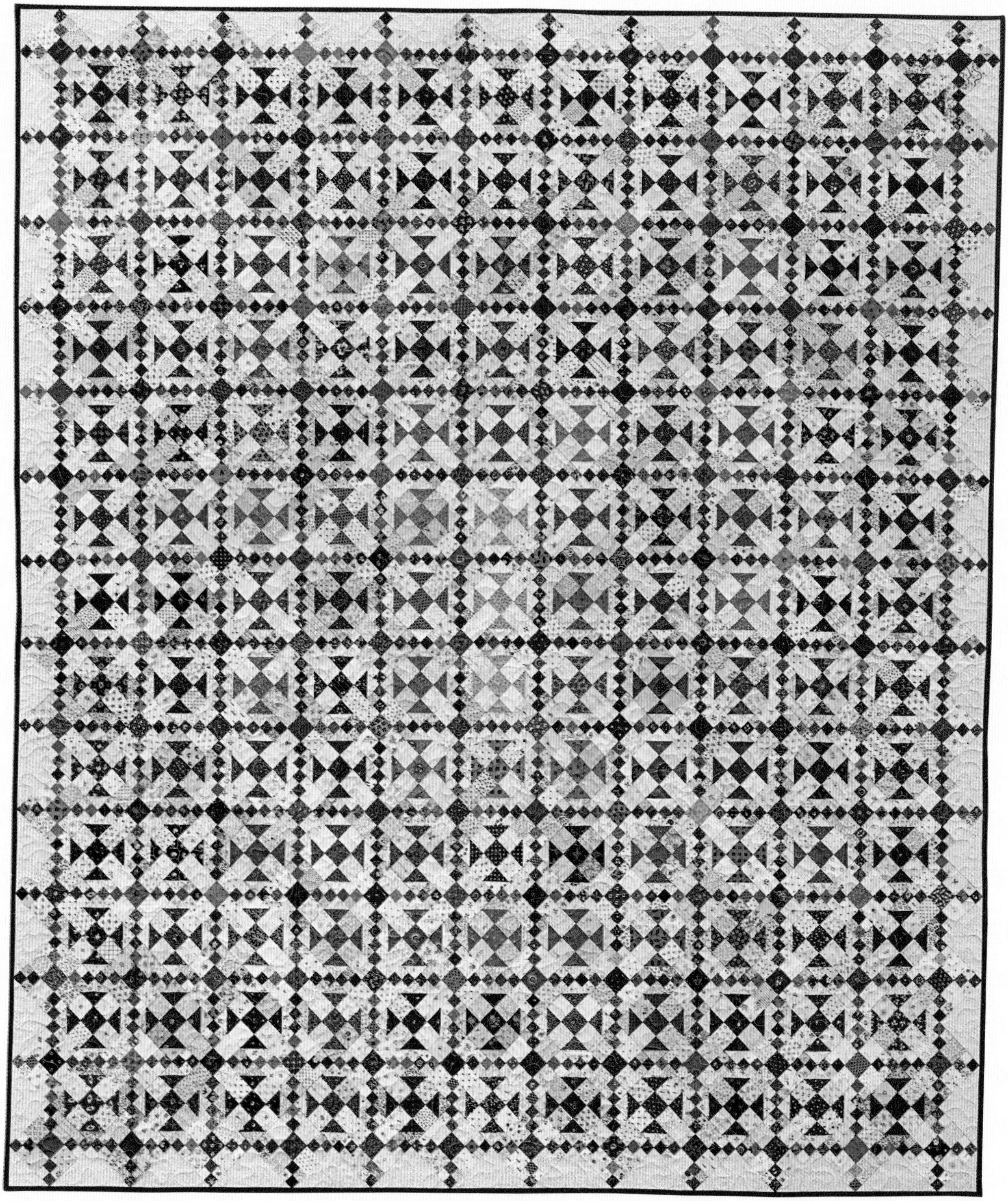

Made by Shelley Scott-Tobisch, quilted by Lauren Tolhurst

The Shoo Fly plant is also known as Apple-of-Peru, so I named this quilt *Appleyard Lane* in honor my great-grandma Ida May Appleyard-Scott.

## FABRIC REQUIREMENTS

*Requirements are based on 40″-wide fabric.*

| PIECE | FABRIC | YARDS |
|---|---|---|
| A, C | Light: all the same or a variety to equal | 2½ |
| F, G | Light: all the same or a variety to equal | 2¾ |
| B, D | Main: all the same or a variety to equal | 1½ |
| E, H | Main: all the same or a variety to equal | 1¾ |
| Side- and corner-setting triangles | Light: all the same or a variety to equal | ½ |
| Binding | Main | ½ |
| Backing | Light or main | 3⅜ |
| Batting | Hobbs Heirloom or equivalent, 90″ wide | 1¾ |

## CUTTING

| FABRIC | PIECE | CUT | SIZE | SUBCUT |
|---|---|---|---|---|
| Light | A | 17 strips | 2¼″ × WOF | 286 squares 2¼″ × 2¼″ |
| | C | 22 strips | 1½″ × WOF | 572 squares 1½″ × 1½″ |
| | F | 34 strips | 1″ × WOF | 68 E/F strips 1″ × 20″ |
| | G | 26 strips | 1½″ × WOF | 672 squares 1½″ × 1½″ |
| | Triangle | 2 strips | 5½″ × WOF | 12 squares 5½″ × 5½″; subcut diagonally twice for side-setting triangles |
| | | 1 strip | 3″ × WOF | 2 squares 3″ × 3″; subcut diagonally once for corner-setting triangles |
| Main | B | 17 strips | 2¼″ × WOF | 286 squares 2¼″ × 2¼″ |
| | D | 6 strips | 1½″ × WOF | 143 squares 1½″ × 1½″ |
| | E | 34 strips | 1″ × WOF | 68 E/F strips 1″ × 20″ |
| | H | 7 strips | 1½″ × WOF | 168 squares 1½″ × 1½″ |

**NOTE:** *I made Appleyard Lane using more than 700 different prints. I organized my fabrics into two piles: lights for the background and darks for the main prints. Then, I placed yellows, oranges, purples, blues, greens, and reds into separate piles. Working through each pile, I began to see my palette emerge. I started with the three yellows in the center and worked out from the center, choosing each round of color depending on my stash. Then, I paired each main print with a coordinating background fabric. I clipped the paired fabrics together, and once all my fabrics were selected, I cut a 2¼″, 1½″, and 1″ strip from each. I added more fabrics from my stash that blended well with all the others for the four-patches. After making the HSTs and four-patches, I worked with Quilt Block Builders, arranging the units in position so I could audition each background fabric before piecing the blocks together. This is such a fun quilt to make. The blocks are portable for retreats, and it makes a fantastic stash buster!*

## CONSTRUCTION

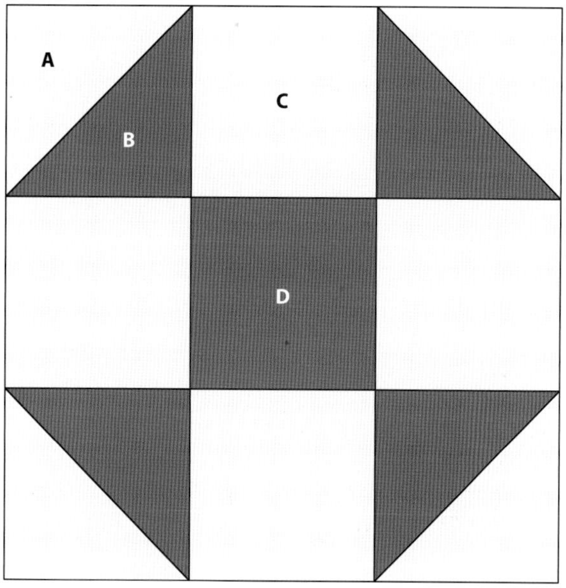


Shoo Fly block

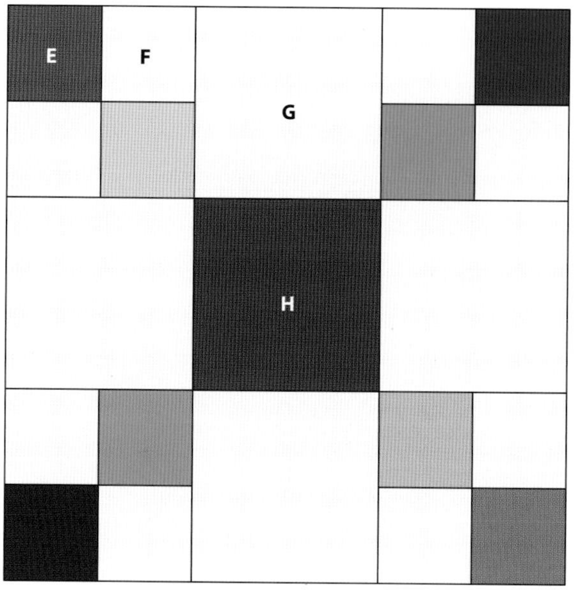


Double Four-Patch block

## Block Assembly

*Before you begin, photocopy the Shoo Fly Quilt Block Builder (page 95) and Double Four-Patch Quilt Block Builder (page 95) and color in the positioning circles to match your clips for color coding (see Positioning Circles, page 10).*

*Note:* Measure your blocks when they are complete. They should be 3½″ square including seam allowances.

### *Piece the HST Units*

*See Making HSTs (page 64).*

1. Make 572 HSTs from pieces A and B.
2. Press the seams toward the main fabric.
3. Trim the HSTs to 1½″ × 1½″.

### *Make the Four-Patch Units*

*See Four-Patch Block (page 53).*

The shorter 20″ strips are easier to work with. They will remain straighter when sewing, pressing, and subcutting. If you are making a scrappy quilt, add variety to your blocks by creating several different E/F strip set combinations.

1. Make 68 E/F strips sets 20″ × 1½″.
2. Subcut into 1,344 strip sets 1″ × 1½″
3. Sew 2 strip sets together.
4. Trim each block to 1½″ × 1½″.

*Note:* Be sure to refer to the Double Four-Patch Quilt Block Builder (page 95) to see which direction to press the seams.

*Make the Shoo Fly Blocks*

**1.** Make 143 Shoo Fly blocks.

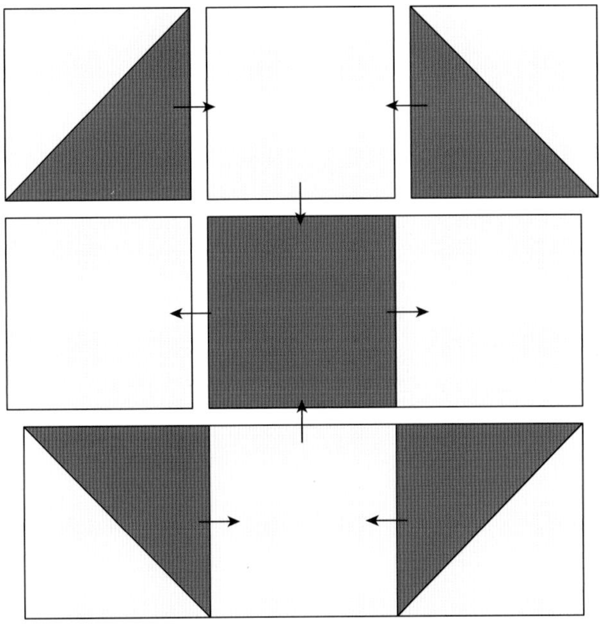

**2.** Make sure the blocks measure 3½″ × 3½″.

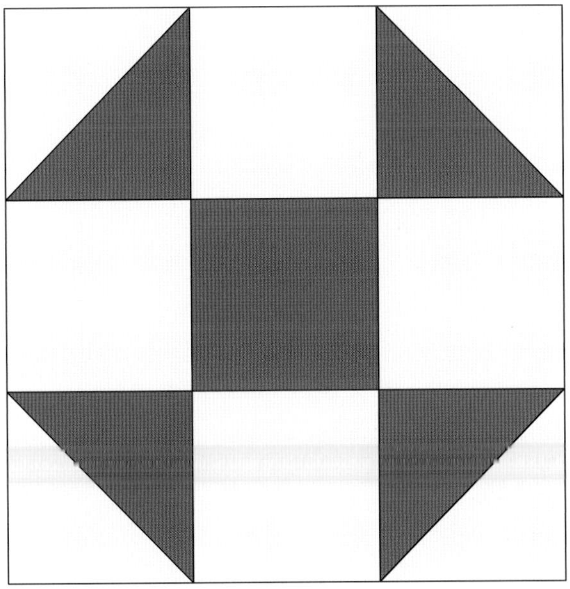

*Make the Double Four-Patch Blocks*

**1.** Make 168 Double Four-Patch blocks.

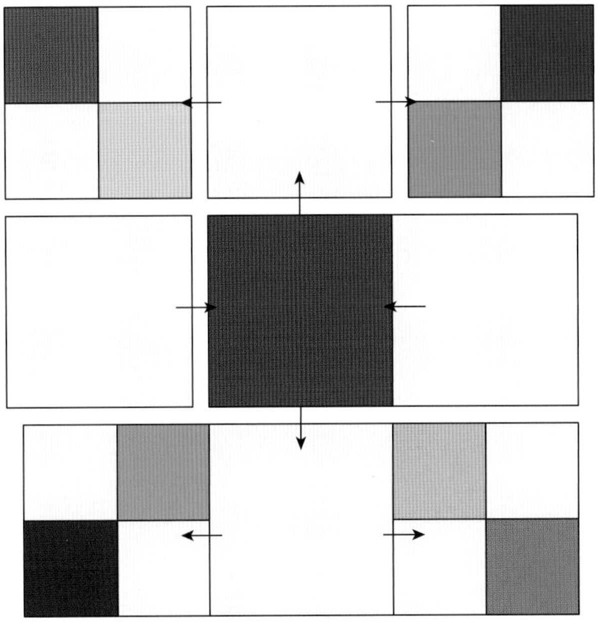

**2.** Make sure the blocks measure 3½″ × 3½″.

## Quilt Assembly

*Arrange the blocks on a design wall if you have one.*

1. Starting at the top left corner, sew the blocks together diagonally in rows, pressing seams toward the four-patches.

2. Add a side-setting triangle to each side.

3. Sew the rows together, pressing seams in opposite directions between each row.

4. Sew the 4 corner-setting triangles on the corners.

## Finish the Quilt

1. Layer the top, batting, and backing (see Backing, page 98) and quilt as desired.

2. Bind and label (see Binding, page 98).

Quilt assembly

Top

Shoo Fly Quilt Block Builder

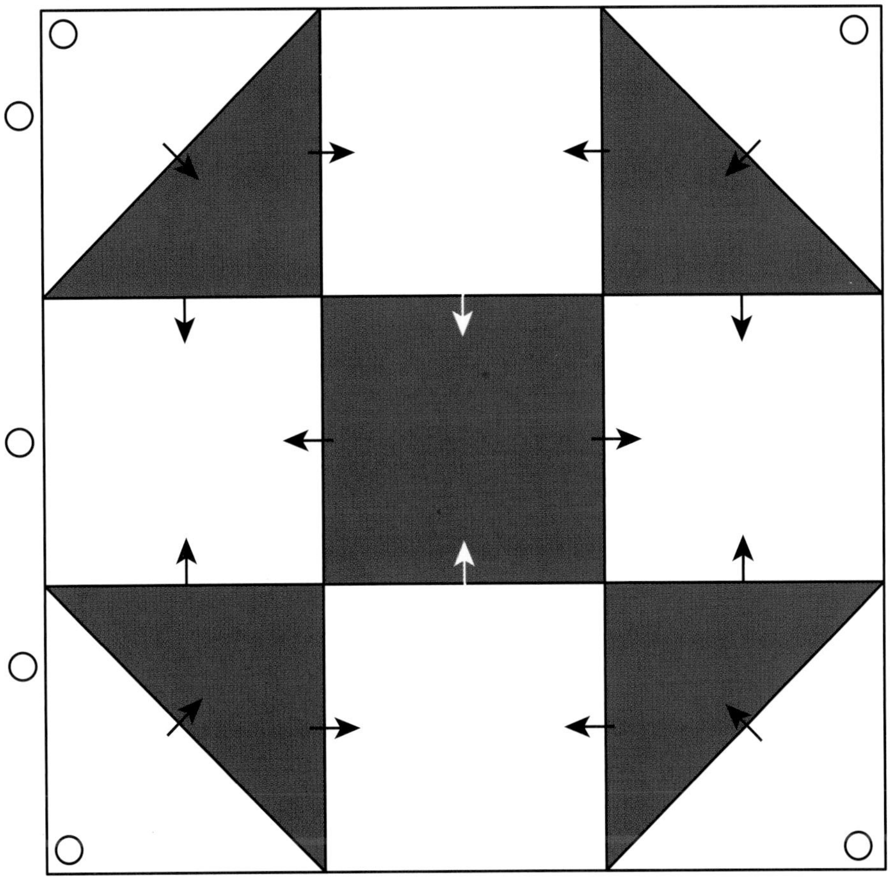

→ Arrows specify pressing direction.

○ Circles within the block indicate where the units belong on the block. Circles outside the block indicate rows to be sewn together.

Top

Double Four-Patch Quilt Block Builder

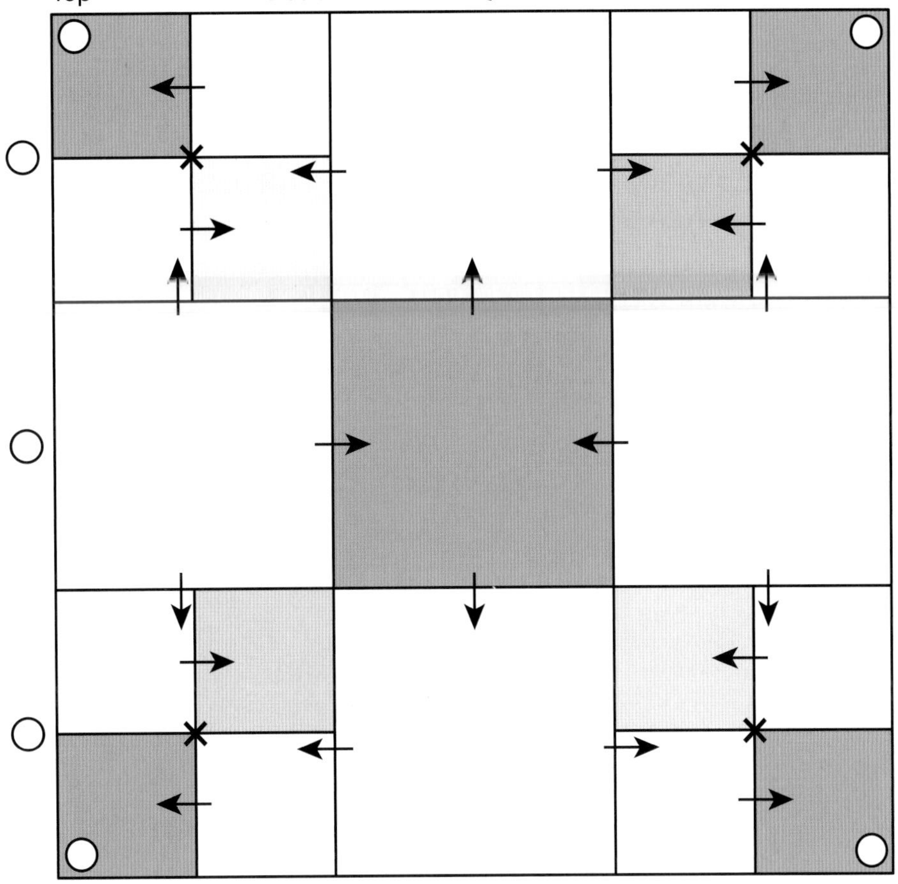

→ Arrows specify pressing direction.

○ Circles within the block indicate where the units belong on the block. Circles outside the block indicate rows to be sewn together.

# BORDERS

Attaching the correct length border is important. I have seen quilt tops that are precisely pieced only to have borders added that are too long. This will result in a quilt with wavy, warped edges that will not hang straight,

## PIECED BORDERS

When adding pieced borders, match and sew the seams using the same precision-piecing methods (page 53) that you use when piecing blocks. To eliminate bulk, sometimes the long seams need to be pressed in opposite directions. See which way the seams naturally fold toward and clip into the seam allowance, right where you want to change the direction of the seam. Clip to *but not through* the stitching. Leave at least two threads intact before the stitching line. Snipping into the seam allowance allows the seams to be pressed toward unpieced blocks, keeps pinwheels sharp at intersections (see *Song of Friendship*, page 82), and maintains a nice flat quilt top. Your borders will be much easier to press and will lie flat.

**NOTE:** *Sometimes you need to use this technique when sewing the quilt top together in rows (see Plum Pudding, page 78).*

## MAKE THE BORDERS

### Measure the Quilt Top

Spread the quilt out onto a flat surface. Make sure the area is large enough to accommodate the entire length and width of your quilt. Measure the quilt through the center from top to bottom. Measure the side edges and the area between the center and side edges.

Measure quilt top.

If all the measurements are the same (rare indeed), this is the length to cut your borders. Usually you will need to determine and cut your borders the average length.

*Find the Average*

To find the average, add the measurements together. For example:

30″ + 30¼″ + 29¾″ + 30¼″ + 29¾″ = 150″

Divide 150 by the number of times you measured, which was 5 in this example:

150 ÷ 5 = 30

Therefore, cut the borders 30″.

*Note:* Use the same measuring tool throughout the entire process from measuring the quilt top to measuring and cutting your borders. Measurements on cloth tapes differ from one another and from acrylic rulers.

**TIP** If your border length is longer than the width of your fabric and you don't want to buy additional fabric to accommodate the longest border, you will need to sew two or more strips together. Sew the strips together using a 45° angle and press the seams open. This will create a nearly invisible, less bulky seam (see Binding, page 98).

## Add the Side Borders

1. Fold the top in half, right sides together, and mark with a pin.

2. Open. Fold the top and bottom to the center and mark with pins.

3. Fold the border strips, wrong sides together, in half and in quarters, and mark with pins.

**TIP** When you fold the border strips in half, fold them wrong sides together and finger press in the seam allowance. The crease will create a little V, making it easier to match to pins along the edge of the top.

4. Center the border strip along the edge of the quilt top. Line up the corners, raw edges, and pins of the border fabric exactly with the corners, raw edges, and pins of the top. Pin border and top together at the marking pins,

5. Ease in any fullness equally between pins.

6. Place little dots of basting glue between pins (see Basting Fabrics Together with Basting Glue, page 43). Press and remove the pins.

7. Sew, backstitching at the beginning and end. Press the seams toward the border.

## Add the Top and Bottom Borders

1. Measure the quilt top from side to side.

2. Find the average and cut your borders.

3. Add top and bottom borders using the same techniques as the side borders.

# FINISHING

## BACKING

Use a print that matches or blends with the fabric in your quilt top. Prewash the backing fabric (see Preparing Fabric, page 24). Measure your quilt top and add at least 8″ to both the length and width measurements. Sew the backing together in three vertical or horizontal panels, rather than down the center. Use a ½″ seam allowance and press the seams to one side. Do not press the seams open as this allows the batting to migrate through the threads and produces a weaker seam.

Avoid center seams when piecing backings.

## BINDING

I use 2″-wide, straight-grain, double-fold binding. I have developed a precise, failsafe, easy technique to sew the ends of the binding together every time without all the measuring.

### Make the Binding

*Determine the Width of Binding Strips*

I prefer to have ¼″ of binding showing on top of my quilt, so I use 2″-wide strips.

To determine the width to cut your strips, choose the measurement you want to see on top of your quilt, multiply that number by 3, and add ¼″ to account for the batting. Double the resulting number to get the cut width.

*Determine the Length of Binding Strips*

Measure the perimeter of your quilt. Add 20″ to account for seams, mitering corners, and sewing the ends together. For example: If the perimeter of your quilt measures 148″, add 20″.

148″ + 20″ = 168″

Divide that measurement by 40, the width of fabric to get the number of strips you need to cut.

168″ ÷ 40″ = 4.2

You can either round up and cut 5 strips 2″ wide to bind the quilt or just cut 4 strips, as the measurement is so close

*Join Binding Strips Together*

*Note:* Do *not* cut the starting end of your binding with a 45° angle. You need a straightedge for this technique.

**1.** Line up 2 binding strips right sides together at a right angle.

**2.** Line up the 45° angle of your ruler along the top edge of the strip.

**3.** Draw a line along the edge of the ruler from the top corner of the ruler to the bottom corner of the fabric.

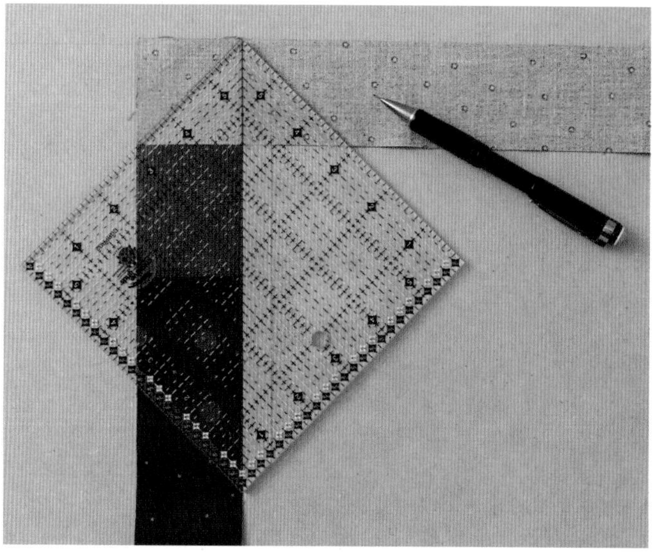

Line up ruler and draw line.

4. Place little dots of basting glue along the outside edges. Press to dry.

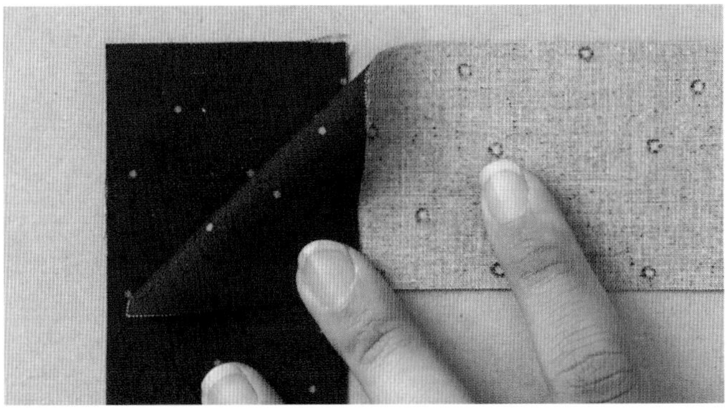

Apply basting glue.

5. Stitch on the line.

6. Trim the seams to ¼″.

Trim the seam.

7. Press the seams open.

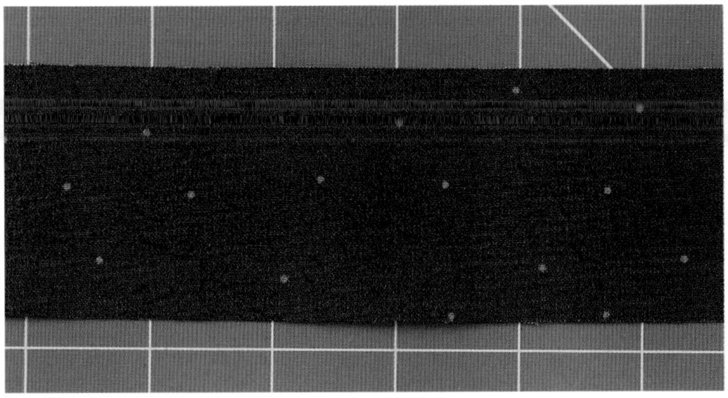

Press the seam open.

8. Press the binding in half lengthwise, wrong sides together, making sure to line up the raw edges exactly.

**TIP** For extra security, place little dots of basting glue in the seam allowance between the two layers and press. This holds the binding layers together, making it easier to attach the binding to the quilt.

## Attach the Binding

Put a walking foot on your machine or use the even-feed mechanism if your machine has one. Set the stitch length to 2 mm or 12 stitches per inch. Use a ¼″ seam allowance.

**TIP** If you have the option to use either a walking foot or an even-feed mechanism, choose the walking foot.

### *Measure the Quilt*

1. Measure all edges of your quilt. Write these measurements down on a piece of paper. Make a note of which measurement is the top, bottom, left side, and right side.

2. Divide the measurements in half and write this number beside the first number. For example:

**Top:** 30″ ÷ 2 = 15″

**Bottom:** 30″ ÷ 2 = 15″

**Left side:** 40″ ÷ 2 = 20″

**Right side:** 40″ ÷ 2 = 20″

3. Mark the center of all 4 edges with a pin.

4. Place the bottom edge of the quilt right side up on your pressing surface.

### *Measure the Binding*

1. Measure 8″ from the edge of the binding and mark with a pin.

2. From the 8″ mark, measure over half the measurement of the bottom edge and mark with a pin.

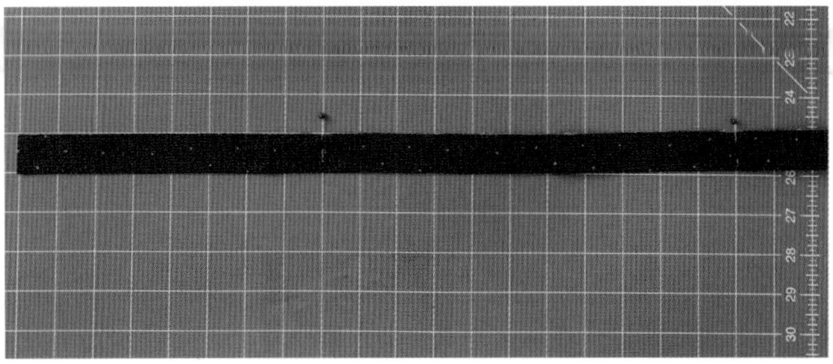

Measure over.

*The First Edge*

Line up the raw edge of the binding with the raw edge of the quilt.

**1.** Match up the 8″ mark on the binding with the center pin on the bottom edge of the quilt.

**2.** Match up the second pin on the binding exactly with the corner of the quilt top and pin or glue in place. Ease in any fullness evenly.

**3.** Mark a dot ¼″ in from the bottom and side edges.

Mark a dot ¼″ in from the corner.

**TIP** I use a Deluxe Corner Trimmer (see ¼″ Marking Tool, page 15) to help find this exact ¼″ measurement. Line up the 90° corner of the ruler with the bottom corner of the quilt. Use a pencil and mark a dot through the hole.

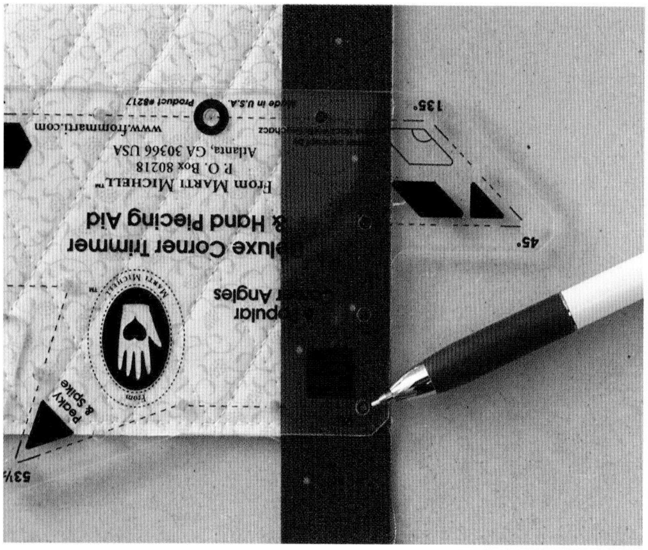

Using Deluxe Corner Trimmer to measure in ¼″

**4.** Begin stitching at the center. (No need to backstitch at this time.) Stitch to the dot, stopping with the needle down directly on top of the dot. Turn the quilt 45° and stitch to and off the corner. Trim the threads and remove the quilt from machine.

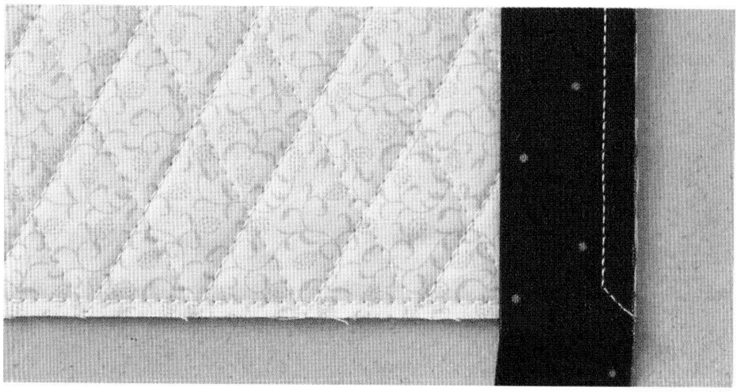

Sew to the dot, and then stitch off at a 45° angle.

*The First Miter*

**1.** Place the quilt so the stitching line is up. Fold the binding away from you, forming a 45° angle.

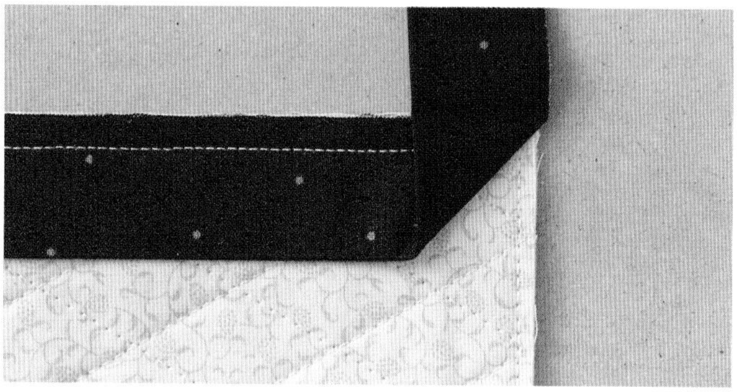

Fold the binding at a 45° angle

**2.** Fold the binding back toward you. Line up the second fold with the upper edge of the quilt. Keep the second fold parallel to and lined up exactly with the top edge. It is here that problems can occur. If the fold is extending beyond the top edge or falls short of the edge you will not achieve a precise miter.

Keep folded binding parallel to and lined up with the top edge.

*The Second Edge*

**1.** Pin the top corner of the binding (including the miter) to the quilt so it will not move.

**2.** Place a pin on the binding at the half and full side measurements.

**3.** Line up the marking pins on the binding with the center and edge of the quilt. Pin or glue the binding to the quilt. Ease in any fullness evenly.

**4.** Mark a dot ¼″ in from the bottom and side edges.

**5.** Start stitching at the top edge of the binding at the fold. Backstitch and continue stitching to the dot. Stitch off the quilt at a 45° angle as with the first edge (previous page).

Backstitch at the beginning of the seam.

**6.** Continue stitching and mitering the binding to all 4 sides. Stop stitching when you are about 12″ from where you started and remove the quilt from the machine.

## Join the Ends of the Binding

*The Set Up*

**1.** Place the quilt right side up on your pressing surface with the bottom edge toward you.

**2.** Cut 2 sticky notes (I prefer Post-it Super Sticky Notes.) the width of the binding × 4″ and mark as shown.

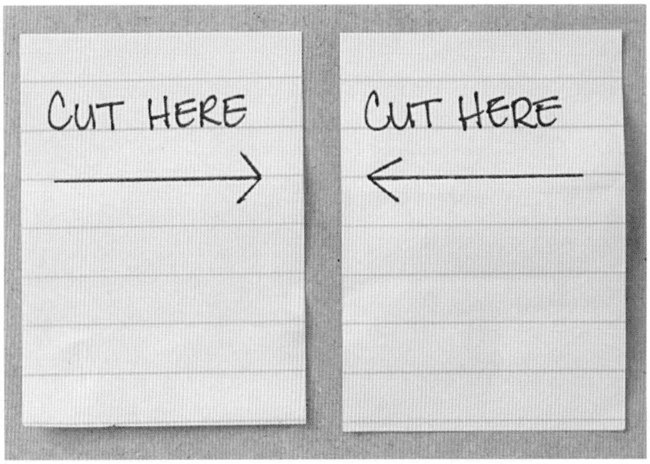


**3.** Position one sticky note about 1″ from the cut end you started with.

**4.** Overlap the other end of the binding on top of the first sticky note, and then place the second sticky note directly above the first.

Overlap the end of the binding.

**5.** Trim the end of the binding that the arrow is pointing to. Slip the corner of a mat under the binding and the first sticky note. Trim binding flush with the Post-it note. Repeat this step for the second sticky note.

Trim the binding.

**6.** Remove both sticky notes and the binding strips will overlap 2″.

### *Sew the Ends Together*

**1.** Unfold the binding strips at both ends. Place the 2 ends right sides together at a right angle. Draw a line from corner to corner at a 45° angle.

Draw line at a 45° angle.

**2.** Stitch on the line, trim the seam allowance to ¼″ and press the seam open.

**3.** Refold the binding and line up the raw edges with the raw edge of the quilt.

**4.** Begin stitching where you left off, overlapping the previous stitches and overlapping the stitches where you started.

## Finish the Binding

**1.** Fold the binding over the edge of the quilt.

**2.** Hand stitch the folded edge of the binding to the back using a blind stitch.

**3.** Miter the corners and stitch them shut for a nice flat finish.

## LABEL YOUR QUILT

Embroider, hand draw using permanent markers, or print your label on printable inkjet fabric sheets. I design my label on the computer and print it out. Hand stitch your label to the back of the quilt.

# ABOUT *the* AUTHOR

**Shelley Scott-Tobisch** discovered her love of quilting after immigrating to Canada from the United States in 1986. The desire to share her passion for quilting led her to begin a teaching career soon after. Shelley's love of scrap quilts, pursuit of precision, and desire to make it more easily attainable led to the development of the techniques and tools used in the Easy Precision Piecing System. It is important to Shelley that her students have success with the techniques taught in her classes. Her focus in class is to ensure that information is presented in such a way that her students can continue to use their newfound skills with confidence.

Shelley and her husband, Bernie (author of *You and Your Sewing Machine*), cofounded Little Oak Pattern Co. Ltd. in 2011. Together they developed the products* for the Precision Piecing System. Shelley and Bernie—a.k.a. "Team Tobisch"—teach classes in the United States and Canada.

When Shelley isn't quilting or teaching, you will most likely find her fishing, either in the lakes around the Boreal Forest in Saskatchewan or down south in the Sea of Cortez, off Baja California.

Shelley lives in a log cabin with her husband in South Surrey, British Columbia, Canada.

** To order the Tobisch products—Quilt Block Builders, Quilt Block Bases, SeamAlign Gentle Hold Fabric Glue, Easy Press Solution, and Easy Press Pen—see Shelley's website.*

**VISIT SHELLEY ONLINE!**

**Website:** easyprecisionpiecing.com • **Blog:** asthespoolturns.blogspot.com